כי נר מצוה ותורה אור

This certificate is presented to

Melissa Goldenberg

for excellence in תורה **studies.**

Camp Mesorah Directors

אחונים

Date:

Camp Rabbi-Educational Director

Assistant Educational Director

קוינדרה

ArtScroll Judaica Classics®

Depth of

Published by

Mesorah Publications, ltd

in conjunction with

ARTSCROLL/Jerusalem, ltd.
ארטסקרול/ירושלים בע"מ

A TVUNAH PUBLICATION

עומק הדין

Judgment

A guide to self-improvement
from the great thinkers of Judaism

by
Rabbi Shalom Meir Wallach

FIRST EDITION
First Impression . . . August, 1991

Published and Distributed by
MESORAH PUBLICATIONS, Ltd.
Brooklyn, New York 11232
in conjunction with
YESHIVAS MIR YERUSHALAYIM

Distributed in Israel by
MESORAH MAFITZIM / J. GROSSMAN
Rechov Harav Uziel 117
Jerusalem, Israel

Distributed in Europe by
J. LEHMANN HEBREW BOOKSELLERS
20 Cambridge Terrace
Gateshead, Tyne and Wear
England NE8 1RP

ARTSCROLL JUDAICA CLASSICS®
DEPTH OF JUDGMENT
© Copyright 1991, by MESORAH PUBLICATIONS, Ltd.
4401 Second Avenue / Brooklyn, N.Y. 11232 / (718) 921-9000

ISBN:
0-89906-948-7 (hard cover)
0-89906-949-5 (paperback

Typography by CompuScribe at ArtScroll Studios, Ltd.
4401 Second Avenue / Brooklyn, N.Y. 11232 / (718) 921-9000

Printed in the United States of America by Noble Book Press Corp.
Bound by Sefercraft, Quality Bookbinders, Ltd. Brooklyn, N.Y.

Publisher's Preface

The masters of *mussar* [ethical thought] have made a major contribution to Torah life in the last hundred and fifty years. Entirely apart from their influence on *yeshivah* education and the countless people who strive to perfect themselves, they have provided new kinds of insight into the interpretation of the Scriptures and teachings of the Sages. It is the last facet of their activity that is the basis of this book.

A primary theme of *mussar* has always been that of judgment. Man tends to live a life of convenience, confident that his deeds are barely noticed by and rarely matter to God. In our emphasis on God as the source of mercy, we tend to forget that He is the Judge, as well. But He *is* — and our deeds *do* matter. To the extent that we recognize this fact and let it penetrate our hearts and minds, we are on the way to improvement and even perfection. Most people focus on this during the Days of Awe, and perhaps the month of Elul. To the thinkers of the Mussar Movement, man's behavior is a vital topic every day of the year, and is the judgment with which it is scrutinized.

That is why the Hebrew edition of this work was so popular. Drawn from dozens of sources, it offers a wealth of insights, stories, and interpretations. It provides an ancedotal portrait of Reb Yisrael Salanter that presents him through his inspiring deeds and incisive understanding of human nature. This is typical of this book's approach. Not only is it stimulating and elevating, it is fascinating nd engrossing reading.

We are grateful to the anthologizer, Rabbi Shalom Meir Wallach, the translator, Yaakov Petroff, and the editor, Yonason Rosenbloom. And to Shmuel Blitz, director of ArtScroll/Jerusalem, who has once again distinguished himself in shepherding this volume to completion. May the readers find it a vindication of all the work and hopes of those who produced it.

Table of Contents

Part One: R' Yisrael Salanter

Part Two:
The Depth of Divine Judgment and Its Causes

Part Three: Reflections by the Masters of Mussar

Part One:
R' Yisrael Salanter

*We are told that the Maharal
of Prague created a golem.
That was a wonder.
But it is an even greater wonder
to create a man from a golem.
That is what the Mussar
Movement does.*

(R′ Yisrael Salanter)

R' Yisrael Salanter

R' Yisrael of Salanter (5570-5643; 1810-1883) was the founder of the *Mussar* Movement. At the age of ten he was giving perceptive and insightful public discourses. At twenty, he served as the head of the *yeshivah* in Salant. At thirty, he was *rosh yeshivah* of one of the famous *yeshivos* in Vilna, the city considered "the Jerusalem of Lithuania." At forty, he stood at the helm of his own *yeshivah*, of a *kollel* of select young married scholars, and of a network of study groups in Kovno. At fifty, he carried his Torah work to Germany — to Halberstadt, Koenigsburg, Berlin, Memel and Frankfurt — and to Paris. At the same time he continued to be involved in communal affairs in Russia, directing his major disciples there. He encouraged and inspired them to put all their efforts into what was most precious to him, the *Mussar* Movement.

His disciples established and directed *yeshivos* throughout Lithuania in which the study of Torah was combined with a program for moral development. Soon, several different schools of *mussar*, each with its unique emphasis, had sprung up — Kelm, Slobodka, Novardhok and others. But what all shared in common was an emphasis on the contemplation of the "depths of Heavenly judgment." In this they followed in the footsteps of the movement's founder, R' Yisrael Salanter.

Let us examine the principles of the *Mussar* Movement to help us understand this emphasis and its consequences.

⮑ Contemplation

*I*n essence, the *Mussar* Movement sought to help a man correct his shortcomings in behavior and character. Failings were defined by any departure or falling away from the demands of the Torah on man. Only the man who acts fully in accordance with Torah is upright: *The commands of Hashem are upright* (*Tehillim* 19:9).

If a man wishes to straighten his ways in the light of the Torah, the first step is to know what the Torah demands. Habit is the great enemy opposing such an examination. Yeshayahu, in his day, voiced his distress with habitual action: *And your fear of Me is a commandment of men which has been learned* (*Yeshayahu* 29:13). Even those who fear Hashem and who study the Torah are chained by convention and the usual patterns of life. They do not subject their every action to ongoing renewed self-criticism.

A few short stories about R' Yisrael Salanter will better illustrate this point.

> A *shochet* who had developed a sense of the fear of God came to R' Yisrael and said that he no longer wished to be a *shochet*. He was concerned lest he unknowingly permit an unkosher animal to be taken as kosher or err in the slaughtering itself. He would thereby cause a loss to the owner. The sense of responsibility weighed heavily upon him.
>
> "Fine!" said R' Yisrael. "But how will you earn a living? After all, you are not built to work at manual labor."
>
> "I thought I would take up teaching," replied the *shochet*. "It is not physically difficult and teachers do earn a living."
>
> "I don't understand," said a puzzled R' Yisrael. "You are worried about causing an improper *shechitah* of an animal. Are you not concerned about possibly causing

damage to the souls of tender children?"

The *shochet* was taken aback and said, "Well then, Rebbe, I'll open a grocery."

"You hesitate to practice *shechitah* lest you commit a single sin involved in improper slaughter," said R' Yisrael, "but you are ready to enter into the business world where you run the risk of thievery, of cheating, of misrepresentation, of using improper weights and measures. Did you know that in the opinion of the *Rambam*, one transgresses the prohibition against improper gain for the slightest sum, even when the amount involved is less than a penny's worth?"

❀ ❀ ❀

On a snowy winter night, R' Yisrael and another scholar reached an inn. The other hurried to the door and held it wide open for R' Yisrael to enter first. R' Yisrael closed it quickly and said, "It is a matter of debate which of us should honor the other. But it is clear that when the door is held open, the warmth escapes from the house. That is a definite case of thievery."

❀ ❀ ❀

A disciple of R' Yisrael invited his master to be his guest at a *Shabbos* meal. The singing and the Torah talk would create an atmosphere of a miniature World-to-Come. R' Yisrael agreed to come.

However, as soon as they had eaten the fish, R' Yisrael asked that the soup be served; as soon as the soup was finished, he asked that the meat be brought. The host did not manage to present any Torah thoughts or sing *zemiros*. The cook was constantly busied with the serving and the removal of the dishes. The host-disciple was bewildered and even angry. This was not the *Shabbos* that he had envisioned.

When R' Yisrael finished the dessert, he asked that the

cook be summoned. "Madam, please forgive me," he said to her, "that I made you weary this evening. Because of me, you were forced to serve the courses one after the other and you had no time to rest between them."

"Whatever are you saying, Rebbe!" said the cook. "May you be blessed with all blessings! I worked without pause the whole day — busy here, cooking there. Now the meal is over I am free to go and rest!"

R' Yisrael turned to his disciple and said, "Did you hear that? Of what worth are all the singing and Torah talk if they in any way deprive a weary servant woman of her rest?"

ᴇᴮ Incorporating Mussar

When one has analyzed the weak points in his character and behavior and when he already knows what the Torah demands of him, then he is faced with a difficult task. He must incorporate that knowledge into his consciousness; his new understanding must be assimilated into his personality and become a part of his nature. How can he do this? There is a single answer: it will only happen through his own strenuous effort.

R' Yerucham of Mir used to say: Our forefather Yaakov was well experienced in the matter of miracles. He divided the Jordan River with his staff; angels who made his herds increase also accompanied him on his return to Eretz Yisrael. Yet when he was informed that his brother Esav was approaching, he prepared himself in three ways — with prayer, with gifts and for war. Why did he not simply request another miracle; that Esav become well disposed toward him? The answer is that Heaven does not intervene in matters which involve a person's character. This is left to man to deal with it himself; that is his purpose in the world, for that he will be rewarded! Thus, Heaven did not change Esav's feelings towards Yaakov.

And how will man manage to accomplish this task? With difficulty and great labor! R' Itzele Peterburger used to say that the verse, *And you shall know today and reflect in your heart that Hashem is God in the heavens above and on the earth below* (*Devarim* 4:39), indicates that the distance between knowing and incorporating this knowledge into the heart is greater than the distance between heaven and earth.

The path is a difficult one, but it is possible. R' Yisrael outlined the path, and its main features comprise the labor of *mussar*.

These features are: emotion, elaboration, and illustration. Let us explain each of these terms briefly.

Emotion: Reason and discernment are the servants of man, but his personality is governed by his heart's will. That is why *Chazal* say that the wicked are possessed by their hearts. Their corrupt will twists their reason and discernment. "The wicked know that their path leads to death, but their loins are covered with fat" (*Shabbos* 31b). The way to pierce through to the heart, to tear through the layer of fat is through the emotions. This can be done by repeating sayings of *Chazal* which arouse the heart to contemplation. We have a living picture of the study of *mussar* by R' Yisrael himself.

> Our master would learn from the texts of *mussar* with great and intense excitement and in a pleasant tone, which would bring on sadness. At times, he would repeat a single sentence over and over with deep emotion. The heart of whoever heard him would melt and turn to water. At times he would weep copiously. Even in old age — when he was sanctified in the extreme, when he was nearly all soul and hardly any sense of the physical remained — he continued to utter the sayings of the *mussar* works with great emotion.
>
> (*Sha'arei Or* ch. 9)

Elaboration: Elaboration fosters emotion. *Chazal* have given us a telling example of this in the *Haggadah*. Its elaborate order is designed to bring us, on the *Seder* night, to the contemplation of Hashem's infinite kindness to us during the Exodus. Nor are we speaking of an intellectual awareness only. For even two scholars are required to ask each other the four questions, to which the required answers detailing the Exodus are given. And even if a man is alone, he is required to ask himself the questions (*Pesachim* 116a). What purpose is there in a man putting questions to himself? The answer is that questions make him focus his attention and incorporate the knowledge gained at a deep emotional level. And the means which *Chazal* use to achieve this absorption by the heart constitute elaboration both in form and in content:

> Had He [Hashem] taken us out of Egypt and not punished them, that would have been sufficient for us. Had He punished them and not their gods, that would have been sufficient for us... How much more so is the good done us multiplied because He took us out of Egypt and punished them and their gods...

The calculations as to how many plagues Hashem inflicted upon the Egyptians in Egypt and how many they received at the Sea, the sketch of Jewish history from Terach, the father of Avraham, down to the enslavement of Israel in Egypt, have one purpose. They are elaboration which arouses emotion. So much for elaboration of content.

But there is also structural elaboration — the format of question and answer. The question stimulates. But it does more than that: it hints at apparently superficial answers. And then when the true answer is given, it makes a far greater impression. The *Mishnah* in *Avos* uses such a technique. It begins by enumerating three qualities which define the disciples of our forefather Avraham and three which define the disciples of the evil Bilaam.

Look at who is being compared: Avraham and Bilaam — light and darkness. And what are the qualities which characterize Avraham? "A good eye, a humble spirit and a lowly soul." "That's it?" one might ask. "Then, perhaps, I have misjudged what I thought to be the enormous gap which separates Avraham from Bilaam." But the *Mishnah* proceeds: What distinguishes the disciples of our forefather Avraham from the disciples of the evil Bilaam? The former eat in this world and inherit the World-to-Come. The latter inherit *Gehinnom* and descend to the pit of destruction.

In short, those three good qualities make all the difference (see *Avos* 5:19).

Illustration: The heart, the will, is not moved by ideas; it is excited by the visual. "The wicked *know* that their path leads to death." But they remain unmoved. To the contrary, at times this very knowledge spurs them on even more to sate their desires: *Eat and drink, for tomorrow we die* (*Yeshayahu* 22:13).

Esav, too, said, "*I am about to die. Why do I need the rights of a firstborn?" And Esav held the birthright in contempt* (*Bereishis* 25:32-34).

And yet, we also find that thoughts of death can help us combat the evil inclination: "If a man sees that his desire is getting the better of him, let him think to himself of the day of death" (*Berachos* 5a). The Alter of Kelm explains how this helps. He stresses the words "to himself" (לו). He suggests that a man should imagine *himself* lying on the ground, the candles burning at his head; next, let him contemplate how he will look as he is placed on the bier and covered with earth. Then the idea will be concrete and it will pierce through from the mind into the heart.

◆§ Maintenance

We have spoken of the means by which the heart may be aroused and developed. But here is the dilemma! This awakening of the heart is prone to dissipate quickly. A man does not change through a single incident, no matter how great an impression it might make. At the dividing of the waters of the Sea, every maidservant saw that which the prophet, Yechezkel, son of Buzi, did not see in his vision of the Heavenly Chariot (see *Mechilta Beshalach on Shemos* 15:2). And the song of praise which followed was a communal prophecy. Nevertheless, Israel fell immediately thereafter: "Their hands held but weakly to the Torah" (see *Sanhedrin* 106a and *Bava Kamma* 82a).

Has there ever been a more impressive or penetrating occurrence than the receiving of the Torah at Sinai — the mountain burning;

darkness, cloud and fog; the tremendous blast of the *shofar*; the voice of the Holy One thundering, *"Do not have any other gods before Me"* (*Shemos* 20:3)? And a mere forty days later, they made the Golden Calf.

This might lead one to be pessimistic and wonder if it is at all possible for man to radically change his ways in a permanent fashion. It was left to a giant like R' Yisrael Salanter to diagnose the source of the difficulty and propose a solution.

The problem exists, as R' Yisrael defined it, because our thought processes and our emotions operate on one plane while our will and our character traits are on another plane. The former operate on a conscious level, while the latter are subconscious. Our labors in the conscious level often do not penetrate to the subconscious.

But such a diagnosis only heightens our dejection. We fear that we shall never succeed in penetrating and rehabilitating the darkness of our inner world.

R' Yisrael, however, also found the solution. He used a common everyday experience by way of illustration. When a child learns to read, he finds the task very difficult. He must learn the shape of each letter, distinguish it from the other letters, learn to combine it with other letters to create a syllable, combine syllables to form an entire word — a complicated course of study which requires exertion and effort. And yet we adults read without being consciously aware of the individual letters which make up each word, without laboring to form syllables, or thinking of the particular meaning of every single word. The ability to read has entered into our subconscious and it operates on its own, so to speak (the same process occurs in learning how to drive and many other such skills). This shows us that constant repetition of ideas, even on a superficial level, will cause these ideas to be implanted into the subconscious.

Fervent study of *mussar* once a week, and continual performance of "exercises" — daily repetition of the major highlights, even if done as a kind of "homework" without a sense of excitement — assures results. And the very lack of depth, the superficiality of the "exercises" is what produces the results. R' Yisrael found support for this idea from the *Midrash*:

What was the beginning of R' Akiva. . .? He was forty years old and had not learned a thing. Once, he stood at the mouth of a well and said: "Who hollowed out this stone?" They told him: "Is it not the water which constantly falls on it day after day?" R' Akiva immediately reasoned: "If the soft cut though the hard, the words of Torah which are as hard as iron will most certainly carve my heart which is of flesh and blood" (*Avos D'R' Nasan* 6:2).

The waters, said R' Yisrael, carved the stone, only because it fell drop after drop for years, without a pause. Had all that accumulated water been poured in a powerful stream at one given instant, it would have slipped off the rock without leaving a trace!

We have a concrete example: that of the Torah itself. It has encompassed us with a web of physical *mitzvos*, which we perform day after day. Most involve a mechanical, unthinking action. It is particularly because they are constant that, without our being aware of it, they shape our character: "The Holy One wished to purify (לְזַכֵּךְ לִזְכּוֹת) Israel. Therefore He gave them Torah and *mitzvos* in great quantity" (*Makos* 23b).

One of the giants of *mussar*, R' Yosef Bloch of Telz, illustrates this point very well: "The *seder* is designed to implant an awareness of the Exodus from Egypt. Had I been asked to do so, I would have suggested an audio-visual show with dazzling effects; a marvelous choir. But *Chazal* chose low-key notes: *matzah*, bitter herbs, *charoses*, the four cups of wine and a long drawn-out recitation of the *Haggadah*. I thought about the matter and understood. Had we been given an impressive show, its effect would have been dazzling, but the impression would have begun to fade on the morrow and would eventually have vanished. It is the low-key notes, the almost indiscernible acts that penetrate; they filter through and find their place in the subconscious. It is they which have an effect.

In this, too, there are levels: One night a year, the night of the *seder*, is entirely dedicated to expanding upon the story of the Exodus, and making it concrete. Elaboration (*the Haggadah*), concretization (the *matzah* and bitter herbs), and illustration ("a man should see himself as if *he* went out of Egypt") are all employed. The *seder* is comparable to the first fervent study of *mussar*. Thereafter, we are commanded to make mention and remember the Exodus in an abbreviated form each morning and evening — this parallels the continuing study of *mussar* which serves to impress ever more deeply until the next exciting occurrence.

We have shown, almost in passing, that all the foundations of the *mussar* movement are anchored in the Torah and its commandments. It did not create a new entity; it only applied these basic Torah attitudes to the area of man's working upon himself and his attempt to improve his temperament and personality.

We have now come to the last principle on our list. It is, in fact, the first in importance and the end purpose of the whole process. This entire work revolves about it.

⋖§ Motivation

We have seen that the way to self-improvement is both penetrating and lengthy. Man must employ both the flame of feeling and the cold unemotional approach implied by constant diligence and restraint. R' Yisrael, himself, commented on this combination of opposites:

> The necessity to labor in tranquility and reach objectives after a long period of time and the desire to reach those objectives quickly are opposing forces. A man must gird himself with both. For if the desire should cease, the efforts will slacken. And should he hurry too much, the labor will almost grind to a halt and, banish the thought, not bear fruit (*Or Yisrael* 20).

Yet, what would drive one to undertake such a difficult and complex task? A man does not work if he does not have an overriding reason which justifies the expenditure of energy. Our complacency indicates that we do not sense the necessity for such profound and demanding labor. Essentially, we are quite pleased with ourselves. Though we are not perfect, the balance sheet, in our minds, shows in our favor.

How can our self-satisfaction be shaken? How can we remove our complacency? We must be shown that this view of ourself is completely false. We do not realize that Heavenly judgment is all penetrating. We have no idea how great is the demand upon us that our deeds be perfect. Nor do we know how far we are from real perfection.

Can this be proven? Who has ascended to the heavens and seen the scales of justice? *Chazal* have done so. The paths of Heaven were clear to them. They enlightened our eyes to see and examine the minuscule failings in the "sins" of the giants of the past, and their consequences — uncompromising punishment. They have not done so to rake over the misdeeds of men of generations gone by, but only so that we should contemplate them and learn from them and thereby motivate ourselves to improve our ways.

In short, a close examination of the depth of Heavenly judgment arouses man to examine his ways — not in the light of the accepted and fashionable, not in the light of the usual and habitual, but by the standards of the Torah perfection which is profound and unbending. "Whosoever says that the Holy One overlooks sins, will have his life overlooked" (*Bava Kamma* 50a).

❀ ❀ ❀

R' Yisrael Salanter only stressed the "fear of punishment." He felt that, although lofty ideas and high-minded thoughts are impressive and moving, man's actual deeds are based on considerations of personal profit. Such is man's constitution and we cannot close our eyes to this reality.

> R' Yisrael did not seek after the great and the wondrous in his talks; he did not speak in terms of the "dread of the transcendent" and "love of Hashem." He spoke solely about the "fear of punishment," for that is the first step in service towards Hashem.
>
> And his source can be found in what *Chazal* have said: "Contemplate three things and you will not come to sin:

know from where you have come, to where you are going, and before Whom you will be making an account — before the King of kings, the Holy One, Blessed is He (*Avos* 3:1).

"The wisest of men, himself, has revealed all this: *Rejoice, young man, in your youth. . . following the path of your heart and the sight of your eyes — but be aware that for all these things, G-d will call you to account* (*Koheles* 11:9). To which *Chazal* have commented: *Rejoice, young man, in your youth* — these are the words of the *yetzer hara* but *be aware that for all these things, G-d will call you to account* —these are the words of the *yetzer hatov* (*Shabbos* 63b).

"The *yetzer hatov* has a single answer to all the seductive arguments of the *yetzer hara* — realization of the future judgment!"

(*Sha'arei Or* 1:10)

In order to inculcate the sense of the fear of punishment, R' Yisrael had to clarify two points — the nature of the punishment and the punishment itself.

Man lives in this world — he will receive his punishment in the World-to-Come. It is his *body* which demands fulfillment of its desires; it is his *soul* which will receive the punishment. It is not that man has any doubts about the punishment or its severity, but he feels detached from that future stage.

That is why R' Yisrael took great pains to repeat and stress in several letters the basic elementary knowledge that:

The essential self, which we can only address by the name "I" (the ego), is the one who speaks, thinks, experiences desire and labors to attain the fulfillment of its desire. It is this "I" hidden in the body which still retains its life force and powers even when the body loses its battle with death. Then, removed from the material world with which it was associated through the body, it will still experience pain and pleasure — terrible, frightening pain or marvelous pleasure beyond compare. That pain and pleasure depend on man's behavior (the behavior of the "I") in this world. Has he heeded the command of Hashem or not? (*Or Yisrael* 6:7,17).

One of the great *kabbalists* (the author of *Leshem, Shevo, VeAchlamah*) once met R' Yisrael and asked him why he did not study *kabbalah*. "What difference does it make to me," answered R' Yisrael, "in which Heaven the Holy One be found? I am certain of one thing. There, they will beat with whips. And it will hurt very, very much. The blows will burn. I am certain of this. Why know more?" (*HaMe'oros HaGedolim* 185).

If one still refuses to understand how it will hurt and why pain will affect the soul, which is spiritual, the Alter of Kelm, the leading disciple of R' Yisrael, explains: The commandments are a demand that man hoe a straight path: *The ways of Hashem are upright* (*Hoshea* 14:10); *The commands of Hashem are upright* (*Tehillim* 19:9); *Elokim has made man upright* (*Koheles* 7:29). When man fulfills the *mitzvos*, he ascends the ladder of perfection. In contrast, when he sins, he becomes distorted and twisted. *See, I have placed before you this day life and the good, and death and the evil. . .and you shall choose life* (*Devarim* 30:15-19). And if, Heaven forbid, he chooses death and the evil, he corrupts his soul, twists it. A soul like that ascends deformed and contorted. But it still contains a good nucleus, it has a Jewish spark to it: it has the vitality of good deeds, the light of *mitzvos*. In Heaven they wish to grant it eternal life — a Divine light, *Gan Eden*. But not in its present state. First, the twisting must be straightened; the bends must be removed. The soul must be weaned away from the corruption. Do we have any idea what pains accompany this process — the repair of a deformation which has become rooted? If we wish to picture such a process, let us look at the pains drug addicts undergo when they break their drug habit! Why do they scream and roar? Why do they want to jump out of their skins or commit suicide? Because there is an attempt to wean them from deep-rooted corruption. We even call their state hell.

⊸§ Let Us Make a Reckoning

However, even one who is conscious of the terrible future punishment and who knows that "he who commits a sin and he who is punished are one and the same," as R' Yisrael put it, is nevertheless tranquil and serene. As we have said, he imagines that his balance sheet shows a credit. What if he has a few little sins? He will come with bundles of *mitzvos* to offset them! R' Yisrael wrestles with this argument also, and, in so doing, reveals a trifle of his genius. He draws up an accounting. Let us follow him, step by step.

There is a basic axiom that for every sort of sin, and at every level of that sin, there is a fitting punishment, specific to it. The idea seems simple and fundamental. Yet even Moshe was shaken when he saw how far ranging this principle was. We are told in the *Midrash* that the Holy One showed Moshe *Gehinnom*. Moshe asked: "Who is judged there?" And He said: "The wicked and those who sin against Me." Moshe began to fear. The Holy One assured him: "I have shown it to you and you shall not pass over to there" (*Bamidbar Rabbah* 23:5).

Of what was Moshe afraid? He was the perfect *tzaddik*; it was he who told all of Israel of the concept of reward and punishment (*Shabbos* 87a). Yet, when Moshe saw how all-embracing judgment is, and how many divisions and sub-divisions there are to *Gehinnom*, he felt fear that he, too, possessed some shade of a failing, a shade of *Gehinnom*. And this, after Hashem had informed him that *Gehinnom* was created for the evil and the sinners!

🦋 🦋 🦋

If there is a whole range of punishments, what determines the severity or leniency of the punishment? The *Rambam* has written:

> This balancing [of sins against worthy acts] is not in accordance to their magnitude. There may be a worthy act which equals several sins, for it is said, *Because a good*

thing was found in him (*Melachim* 14:13). And there is a sin which equals several worthy deeds, for it is said, *a single sinner will destroy much good* (*Koheles* 9:18). And the balancing is only with the Divine wisdom of the G-d of Knowledge; He knows how to measure worthy acts against sins (*Hilchos Teshuvah* 3:2).

Yet, *Chazal* teach us how to weigh our acts. They have said: "One with pain is better than one hundred without" (*Tanna D'vei Eliyahu*). A *mitzvah* performed with suffering, by shattering sloth and overcoming the desire to avoid discomfort, is rewarded a hundredfold.

Just as the suffering is taken into consideration in Heaven with respect to the reward of a *mitzvah*, so too, the difficulty in opposing one's evil desire is a factor which is taken into account when punishment is meted out. The easier it was to overcome one's desire, the more one will be punished for failing to do so. For example, in antiquity, one of the strands of *tzitzis* was dyed blue by the blood of the *chilazon*, which was very rare and expensive. If two men wore *tzitzis* on their garments and one, out of laziness, neglected to have the blue strand and the other neglected to have the undyed white strands, the *Gemara* tells us that the punishment of the one who lacks the white strands is greater than that of the one who lacks the blue.

A parable is given by way of illustration. A king ordered one servant to bring a seal (signifying slave status) of clay and another a seal of gold, and both failed in their duty. Who receives the greater punishment? The one who did not bring the seal of clay (see *Menachos* 43b).

Two men commit the same sin. In one, the flame of the evil desire burned fiercely, so that he could not stand against it; he fell and sinned. He will, indeed, be punished. Yet, his punishment will be far less than the other who might easily have overcome his desire, but did not fight against it at all. With each declining level of desire, the severity of the punishment rises a hundredfold and more!

Punishment is meant to be a deterrent. If so, then it must be more severe than any suffering which would be the result of not committing the sin. For example, no body of legislators would pass a law that the punishment of a thief is, merely, to return that which he has stolen. Such a punishment would not deter a man from stealing. Only if the thief must pay twice what he has stolen, or be cast into jail and beaten, is the punishment a deterrent.

If we apply this example to our discussion, we must take another factor into account. Were we to say to a thief that he must pay twofold of what he has stolen — fifty years from now, that would not be a deterrent. Since the punishment of sin is held in store for the future, we must assume, if it to be effective, that it is far, far greater than the suffering caused by refraining from the sin.

❦ ❦ ❦

How much pain does the Torah demand that we suffer in order to avoid a sin? This will give us a yardstick to determine how terrible the punishment will be, if we succumb to desire and trespass.

A man must give up all his possessions in order to avoid sinning (*Rama, Shulchan Aruch, Yoreh Deah* 157:1). The Gaon of Vilna notes that this applies even to transgressing a rabbinical ordinance with respect to *Shabbos* and he refers to a *Mishnah* as proof. We are told that if a fire breaks out on *Shabbos* we are not to expressly tell a non-Jew to extinguish it, even though commanding a non-Jew is only prohibited by rabbinic decree (see *Shabbos* 121a and *Rashi* ad loc.).

A man sees his home and all his worldly goods going up in smoke! He will not have a roof·over his head or bread to eat. He, his wife and children will be in the street in need of everything; they will be destitute. And he can avoid all this with a word; a word that will "only" be a transgression of a rabbinical law. But he will not say that word to the non-Jew. He chooses to live a life of poverty rather than sin. For such is the law.

What prevents him from murmuring that little word and saving his worldly goods? It is because he knows that if he does say it and does transgress, he will receive a punishment ten times more dire than the poverty of a lifetime which hangs over him and his family.

Were he to speak that one word and transgress, would he not

have a justifiable excuse when he appears before the Heavenly court? Would he not be able to say: "It was almost as if I had been compelled against my will; I was confused and troubled; I saw everything going up in flames before my eyes and I pictured a life of want and poverty; the goods of others were in my trust. I couldn't contain myself and told the gentile to put out the fire!"

His argument is taken into consideration in Heaven and his punishment is reduced a hundredfold with the difficulty to be experienced in overcoming the urge to order the gentile to put out the fire. Nevertheless, when all is said and done, a punishment still remains, compared to which a life of suffering for him and his family would be as nothing!

What, then, would be the punishment for a transgression in matters ordained by the rabbis, where it is easily possible to overcome the urge?

And if this is the punishment for a rabbinic prohibition, what, then, for transgressing a Torah commandment?

One further example. We are told of a young, refined woman whose husband left the house and disappeared. She falls into the status of an abandoned wife, who is forbidden to remarry. Two witnesses arrive and testify that they saw her husband dead. Marvelous! Her restraints have been removed. But, then, two other witnesses arrive and say that they saw her husband alive. Two against two! A terrible predicament. She cannot be permitted to remarry.

Now what if the woman is herself certain that her husband has died; if she, too, has seen him dead? As far as she herself is concerned, she is ready to remarry without a qualm. And one of the witnesses who said that he saw her husband dead, with his own eyes, is ready to marry her. What is the ruling? If the act has not yet occurred (i.e. if she has not remarried), she should not do so. The sages have so decreed, because a cloud hangs over the issue. But if she has remarried, the marriage may be upheld (see *Kesubos* 22b).

A young woman stands before a terrible trial. She is certain, she knows, that her husband is dead. The man who wishes to marry her saw her husband dead. Here, she has an opportunity, on the one hand, to rebuild her life, to establish a family, or choose a life of solitude, with its dark nights of loneliness, through to a barren old age. And all in order to avoid overstepping a rabbinical prohibition, which is only effective before the act.

If she does not withstand the temptation, the punishment which awaits her there, in the World-to-Come, is far worse than the fate of being an *agunah* for seventy years, even though the difficulty of the trial would be taken into consideration in determining the punishment.

Is is forbidden to transgress *Shabbos* or another Torah prohibition to save a part of the body where there is no danger to life involved (*Shulchan Aruch, Orach Chaim* 328:17). Let us picture for ourselves a man who suffers from a disease of the eyes which threatens to bring on blindness. He is told that he can prevent blindness by eating forbidden food once. He is not allowed to do so. He must accept his impending blindness with eyes open, as it were. It is impossible to estimate the reward that will be his for remaining firm in the face of the ordeal. But if he succumbs, eats the forbidden food and becomes well, he must look forward to a terrible punishment, one worse than an entire lifetime spent in blindness. And this, despite the great pressure which drove him to eat from the prohibited food. True, that pressure is taken into consideration and his punishment is held to the minimum. That minimum, however, is worse than the experience of living a lifetime as a blind man of whom *Chazal* say, "A blind man is like a dead man."

Let us modify the picture. It is not a lifetime of blindness which hangs over him but a shorter period — ten years. That, too, is a cup of bile, but it cannot be compared to a lifetime of blindness. We can assume that if he ate the prohibited food in such an instance, his punishment would be many times more severe than in the first case. For he has not withstood a lesser trial. And if the ordeal were "only" a year's blindness and he succumbed and ate the forbidden, his punishment would be far, far greater, although this, too, would be a terrible ordeal — three hundred and sixty-five days of blindness.

If, on the other hand, one oversteps a prohibition of the Torah, let us say, against idle talk, malicious gossip, or causing discomfort to his fellow, without rhyme or reason, without any compulsion such as the threat of blindness, his punishment will be infinitely more severe than that of a man who acts under the threat of a lifetime of blindness. Can anyone, now, truly say that he will ascend to the next world with a quiet heart because the scales show a weight in his favor?

The principles of the *Mussar* Movement made their impression on the entire manner of thinking of recent generations. At first, many hesitated to come under the tent of those who made much of soul-accounting and spoke of the awesome aspects of punishment. They were wary lest this would lead to depression and discouragement. R' Yisrael Salanter did not agree with them. As he put it:

> I have seen a soldier, derelict in his duty, receive his quota of blows in punishment, rise, and carry on. He did not have time for worry and depression. A Jew is a soldier in the service of the Creator. The "blows," which *mussar* rains upon him, aid him in improving his ways. Where can he find the time to be sad?

Of those who avoid studying *mussar* lest they experience fear, he said:

> They are like a man who, although he is afraid of thunderstorms and is concerned lest he be struck by the lightning which accompanies it, does not set up a lightning rod. Instead, he huddles under the covers and buries his head in the pillows so as not to hear the claps of thunder...

When R' Yechezkel Levenstein was once asked if *mussar* leads to depression, he replied, "If man is shown his faults, and is taught how to correct them and perfect himself, I cannot see how *melancholia* can enter the picture."

And the Alter of Novardhok said to one of his disciples, "In the course of my entire life, I have met but one truly happy man: R' Yisrael Salanter."

Part Two:
The Depth of Divine
Judgment and Its Causes

The Depth of Divine
Judgment and Its Causes

✒ The Obligation to Contemplate
the Depth of Divine Judgment

The Alter of Kelm found the obligation to contemplate the depth of Divine judgment in a passage of Tractate *Kiddushin*.

If a man unintentionally uses a sacred object and derives a penny's worth of benefit, he must return the value of whatever enjoyment he has derived, plus an additional fifth of that amount. In addition, he must bring a guilt-offering worth at least two *sela'im*. *Chazal* comment, "Calculate how many *perutos* there are in two *sela'im* — close to two thousand." And *Rashi* adds, "Contemplate how much a person should strive to distance himself from a sin. Even for an unintentional sin [from which he derived such slight benefit], he must bring such a great expiation" (*Kiddushin* 12a).

From this we learn that a man is obliged to contemplate the Divine punishment in all its details.

It is fear of punishment which moves us to fulfill the entire Torah and its *mitzvos*. In addition, the fear of Hashem is a *mitzvah* in its own right:

> The fourth *mitzvah* is that He has commanded us to believe in His awesomeness and to be afraid of Him, and not be like heretics who walk in the obstinacy of their hearts, viewing the events of the world as happenstance. Rather, we should fear *His punishment* at all times, as it is explicitly commanded in the verse (*Devarim* 6:13): *Hashem, your G-d, you shall fear* (*Rambam, Sefer HaMitzvos*).

But how can we understand Divine punishment? Have not *Chazal* said that the depth of judgment is hidden from the human eye (see *Pesachim* 54b)? For that very reason, when we are given the opportunity to view some aspect of His judgment, we are obligated to contemplate that closely. That is why the *tanna* points out that even one who sins unintentionally, and derives but a *perutah*'s worth of benefit, he must still pay close to two thousand times the value he may have derived from the sanctified object, even though he has already repented.

But that is only the first stage of the calculation. A man spends close to two thousandfold so that he will be spared punishment in the world above. Is there a difference between the payment and the punishment which it erases? Yes! There is a vast difference. For in our world, the Holy One joins His aspect of mercy to that of justice (*Bereishis Rabbah* 12:15). However, the world above is a world of justice only; mercy and justice do not co-exist there. That is why the fire of *Gehinnom* is hotter than our fire by sixty times (*Berachos* 67b), and, as the *Rambam* writes, the lightest punishment there is worse than all the suffering of Iyov. That is what is meant by justice!

Imagine what the punishment will be if we come to that world above without having repented. If the expiation in this world, even after *teshuvah*, is close to two thousandfold for an unintentional sin, then, how great must the future punishment be for a sin done without intent when the sinner does not repent.

(*Chochmah U'Mussar* I: *Ma'amarim*)

❁ ❁ ❁

Thus far, we have only dwelt on the punishment of a single, isolated sin for which the sinner did not repent. But when a man sins a second time, his punishment is worse than it was for the first offense. For the sin thereby becomes rooted in his soul, so much so, that *Chazal* said, "When a man sins and repeats that sin, the sin itself becomes in his eyes a permissible act. From that point on, he is punished even only for his thought to commit the sin" (*Kiddushin* 40a).

Chazal tell us that whoever commits a sin unintentionally is viewed as an intentional sinner when he repeats the same sin unintentionally (*Beitzah* 16a). What, then, are we to think of the man who transgresses intentionally a second time? A third time?

Place a grain of wheat on the first square of a chessboard, two on the second, four on the third, sixteen on the fourth, and with each subsequent square multiply each previous number by itself. Even the treasure vaults of a king could not supply coins equal to the number of grains of wheat needed for square sixty-four (the tenth square alone would require 3,500,000,000,000 grains)! Well, then! What if the sin was committed more than sixty-four times, and with each successive time the severity of the punishment is more than squared? Nor is the punishment of the first transgression as light as a grain of wheat; we are to be burned by the fires of *Gehinnom*.

Small wonder that *our sins have become so numerous that they are higher than our head*, that *our guilt has grown to the heavens* (*Ezra* 9:7).

(*Chochmah U'Mussar* II:284)

❧ ❧ ❧

In brief: *Chazal* wished to teach us that after a sin of the lowest level of blame (an unintentional sin), of the slightest extent (a *perutah's* worth of benefit), with the lightest possible sentence (in this world where justice is tempered with mercy), when all mitigating factors are taken into consideration (i.e. return of the value used, plus the fine of one-fifth of that value, and after *teshuvah*), a man must still bring a sacrifice which is worth almost two thousand times the value of unlawful use.

Far, far greater will be the consequences in the Upper World where mercy has no place. We have no comprehension of how severe punishment is there!

Nevertheless, we can at least set bounds to this "no idea" of ours, following the lead of the Alter of Kelm.

The Torah tells us: *For Hashem will not cleanse the one who takes His name in vain* (*Shemos* 20:7). *Chazal* elaborate, "The Heavenly court does not hold him guiltless; the earthly court, nevertheless, punishes him with flogging and cleanses him of guilt" (*Temurah* 3a-b). The author of the *Shitah Mekubetzes* claims that *Chazal* meant to tell us far more than that Hashem does not compromise with respect to this sin. That is self-evident. The Holy One does not ignore sins, and "whosoever says that the Holy One overlooks sins will have his life overlooked" (*Bava Kamma* 50a). Rather, the Torah is teaching us that punishments executed by the human court, such as thirty-nine stripes, do cleanse. But if one is subject to flogging in Heaven, then "Hashem will not cleanse"; that person will be flogged and flogged, ceaselessly (for Heaven is the world of eternity and a part of eternity is also eternity).

But, perhaps, it might be argued, such eternal punishment applies only to the heinous sin of using Hashem's name in vain. That is not so. Chazal have said that when the Torah says of the Holy One: *He will cleanse, He will not cleanse* (*Shemos* 34:7), this means that He will pardon those who repent and not pardon those who do not repent (*Shevuos* 39a). For overstepping a prohibition, only once, he will be flogged in Heaven endlessly.

We have no conception of what a Heavenly flogging is. But we do have some idea of flogging in this world of ours. *Chazal* say that if Chananiah, Micha'el and Azariah, who were willing to sacrifice their lives for the sake of Hashem and be thrown into the fiery furnace, had been flogged instead, they would have succumbed and bowed down to the idol (*Kesubos* 33b). Flogging without end is more difficult to bear, it seems, than death by fire. And that is the punishment which awaits the one who has not repented each and every sin which he has committed.

Teshuvah can remove the sin and save us from such punishment. How we should rush to repent!

(*Chochmah U'Mussar* I:225).

R' Aharon Kotler contemplated the terrors of punishment as revealed through the laws of going to war.

The Torah says: *And the officers shall add ... and say, "What man is there who is fearful and soft of heart? Let him go and return to his home"* (*Devarim* 20:8). R' Yosi HaGalilee explains that the "fearful" man, to whom the Torah refers, is one who is afraid because of the sins in his hand. And the *Gemara* says that this includes even one who commits a sin of rabbinic origin. An example is given of such a sinner: one who spoke between putting the *tefillin* on his arm and putting the *tefillin* on his head. By talking, he has separated the *mitzvah* of the *tefillin* of the hand from that of the head, and the blessing he made before starting to put *tefillin* on his arm cannot now apply to the *mitzvah* involving the *tefillin* for the head. If he does not make a new blessing prior to placing the *tefillin* on his head, he transgresses (see *Sotah* 44b; *Menachos* 36a). And he must withdraw from the line of battle, lest he die because of this sin (*R' Eliyahu Mizrachi*).

The transgression is only rabbinic — virtually all blessings are of rabbinic origin. Nor did he completely neglect to pronounce a blessing, having made one when he put the *tefillin* on his arm. Had he not spoken before putting on the *tefillin* of the head, that blessing would have been valid for both *tefillin*. Moreover, his transgression was unintentional: he thought that the blessing he had made still applied. Nevertheless, the sin is so terrible that he ought to fear, lest he fall in battle because of it.

And what of a full-fledged rabbinical transgression committed with intention? And what of a sin found in the Torah? And what of a sin for which it is expressly stated that we deserve death — e.g., neglecting the study of Torah? There we are told: He who does not learn, deserves death (*Avos* 1:13).

❧ The Greatness and Loftiness of the Holy One

R' Yerucham of Mir throws light on another aspect of the depth of judgment.

David says, *You are awesome Elokim from Your Temples,* מִמִּקְדָּשֶׁיךָ (*Tehillim* 68:36). *Chazal* read מִמִּקְדָּשֶׁיךָ as מִמְּקֻדָּשֶׁיךָ — not as "Temples" but as "the holy ones in the nation." They understand the verse to mean that when the Holy One passes judgment and punishes the righteous, he is feared, elevated and praised (*Zevachim* 115b).

We recognize the transcendence of the Holy One when He metes out justice. *And Hashem of Hosts is uplifted — in judgment* (*Yeshayahu* 5:16). Judgment is the source from which "Hashem of Hosts is uplifted."

> *And it was on the third day, at daybreak, and there were sounds and lightning and a thick cloud on the mountain and a very strong sound of the shofar* (*Shemos* 19:16). The Torah was given in the morning and the laws in the evening. That is what is written: *From morning to night they will be crushed* (*Iyov* 4:20). Imagine two men who have been condemned to be flogged (because they produced a flawed object): one of them is a craftsman, the other not. Why is the non-artisan to be flogged? Because he had no one to teach him. In such fashion did the Holy One stand on Sinai and hold [to the course of] justice. As it is stated: *And My hand takes hold of justice* (*Devarim* 32:41).
>
> David said, *Hashem, judge me in accord with my righteousness* (*Tehillim* 7:9). He searched and did not find anyone to teach him and he was flogged. He began to cry out (*Tehillim* 143:2): *And do not come to Your servant with justice* (*Shemos Rabbah* 30:11).

Before he was flogged and shown "justice," David thought of himself as righteous and requested Hashem to "judge me in accord with my righteousness." But after the flogging, he recognized the strictness of the judgment and he cried out, "Don't come to Your servant with justice, for no mortal can be righteous before You."

The *Midrash* goes on to say that Iyov, too, thought that he understood justice until he experienced reward and punishment:

> [Iyov] is compared to a drunk hooligan who stoned the statue of the ruler, cursed the authorities and said, "Show me where the ruler is and I'll teach him a lesson." He entered and they showed him the ruler seated on his throne. [The ruler] imprisoned a noblewoman, banished an earl, punished a duke with blindness and had a count beaten. When [the hooligan] saw this he became frightened and said, "Pardon me, I beg of you, I was drunk and did not realize the extent of the ruler's power."
>
> And in a like manner, Iyov stood and cried out, *Oh that I knew where I might find Him... and I would arrange my cause before Him* (*Iyov* 23:3-4).
>
> He stoned the statue — i.e., he said, *May the day on which I am born be lost* (*Iyov* 3:3). (By cursing himself, he cursed the image of G-d that was within him.)
>
> (*Shemos Rabbah* 30:11)

Suddenly, he saw the ruler on his throne decreeing imprisonment for a woman of highest nobility. This was the prophetess, Miriam, who was punished with leprosy for a sin committed with good intentions; she wished to save her sister-in-law from being left husbandless (after Moshe separated himself from her). In Heaven, she was judged guilty of speaking maliciously and punished with leprosy. This shows us the depth of Divine judgment.

He banished an earl. This was Moshe who was not allowed to enter the Holy Land, but died in the desert for a sin so slight that the commentators weary themselves trying to explain it. *Chazal* say that if Moshe had entered the Land, Israel would never have gone into exile; and Moshe would have been the *Mashiach*.

The Holy One is elevated by such dire punishment: *For who will be righteous before You* (*Tehillim* 143:2). When we see that no one is righteous, then we understand what "before You" means.

He punished a duke with blindness. This is Yitzchak whose eyes became dim.

He decreed that another suffer exile and backbreaking labor. This was Avraham. Because he said, *"With what shall I know,"* (*Bereishis* 14:8) he was told, *Know, indeed, that your children will be strangers in a land not their own and they will work them and torment them for four hundred years* (ibid. 14:13).

> When Iyov saw the power of judgment, he said, "Forgive me, I beg of you, I was drunk," as it says, *If truly I erred, let my error rest upon me* (*Iyov* 19:4). And why did so much occur? Because they did not know the power of judgment (*Shemos Rabbah* ibid.).

Until he saw Divine judgment being executed, Iyov thought that he had reached the pinnacle of understanding. Thus he said, "I will arrange for justice before Him." He imagined that he was aware of the full glory of the Creator. But that was before he witnessed the true judgment and saw that even a shadow of a sin was punished. And he realized the error: the failure to comprehend "before Whom" the sin is committed. He then looked deep within himself and saw how distant he was from perfection in his service before so lofty a G-d. Then he said, "Pardon me, I beg of you, I was drunk, I was in error, it was unintentional." Then he understood that there are no bounds to Hashem's greatness, no limit to His loftiness, and that man can never fulfill his obligations of service towards Him. This he learned only from witnessing Divine judgment, which takes into account even the slightest of sins.

(*Da'as Chochmah U'Mussar* I:79)

ᴇᔐ Hashem's Judgment Is on Each Aspect of the Sin

R' Yechezkel Levenstein, the *mashgiach* of Mir and later Ponevezh, stressed two points with reference to Heavenly justice. The lack of awareness of these two points leads one into a false complacency.

The *Ramchal* stresses that man is punished for every sin, no matter how slight. Just as justice must take into account every *mitzvah*, so too, it cannot ignore any sin.

Yet, even when a man knows that he will be punished for every aspect of his sins, he still thinks of his transgressions in only a general fashion. He knows, for example, that when he prays without the proper intent, he will be punished. But does he consider that this punishment will be for each word, each letter, for each blessing, each of the Holy Names which he uttered without the proper intent. The *Zohar* says we deserve death at the hands of Heaven for every Holy Name which we pronounce without the proper thoughts.

A man knows that he will be punished for neglecting his Torah study: "He who does not learn deserves death" (*Avos* 1:13). But he does not consider that a single day is made up of hours and the hours made up of minutes and in the space of a minute, it is possible to learn two hundred words. He deserves the death penalty for each possible word which he might have learned.

> The *Midrash* relates:
>
> Come and see the difference between Moshe and Shmuel. Moshe would enter [the *Ohel Moed*] and come before the Holy One to hear what was said. But with respect to Shmuel, the Holy One came to him: *And Hashem came and stood* (*Shmuel I* 3:10). Why was this so?
>
> The Holy One said, "I act towards man with justice." Moses would sit and those who required judgment would come to him and be judged: *And Moshe sat to judge the*

nation (Shemos 18:13). But Shmuel traveled to each area to judge the people so that they need not trouble themselves to come to him: *And he went every year and encircled Beis El and Gilgal and Mitzpah and judged Israel in all these places (Shmuel I* 7:16). The Holy One said, "Moshe who sat in one place to judge Israel shall come to the *Ohel Moed* to hear what is to be said. Shmuel, however, went to Israel, to the towns and judged them; I will go and speak with him" *(Shemos Rabbah* 16:4).

Should Moshe have gone to all the far-flung corners of Israel? Certainly not! There was no place to which to travel; Israel was all concentrated in the desert. If he had been faced with the same situation as Shmuel, with Israel spread out over the face of the Land, Moshe, too, would have gone to them. Why then should his prophecy be given in an inferior manner to that of Shmuel?

The precision of Divine reward is equally great, as the *Midrash* indicates with respect to Yehudah: "Because he [Yehudah] saved three souls, Tamar and her two sons from the fire, the Holy One saved his three sons from the fire. And who are they? Chananiah, Micha'el and Azariah" *(Shemos Rabbah* 16:4).

More than a thousand years passed before the reward was given. But there is an additional puzzle here. Did such a deed deserve a reward at all? If Yehudah had remained silent and allowed his daughter-in-law and future sons to be burned, that would have been a grave sin. By confessing, he did no more than he should have. Why, then, did he deserve such a reward? His descendants were saved from a fiery furnace which had been heated for seven days, and an angel was sent from on high to rescue them.

Every deed produces either reward or punishment. Moshe did not move from his place; so, too, the Divine Presence did not move for him. Yehudah saved Tamar and her unborn twins from fire, and as a consequence, his descendants were saved from fire.

❧ ❧ ❧

The *Midrash* defines these principles of Divine justice by applying the verse: *Hashem has a level and scales of justice (Mishlei* 16:11). The *level* and *scales* represent one principle, namely that justice is administered with very fine calipers, down to a hairsbreadth. *Hashem* is the second principle: Hashem's justice is of a completely different order. His justice overlooks not a single act or part thereof, and each causes a Divine reaction for good or evil (*Or Yechezkel*, Elul 18-20).

❧ Dividing the Deed into Its Component Parts

R' Chaim Zaitchik, the *rosh yeshivah* of the Novardhok yeshivah in Butchatch, points out that we tend to see a sin as an undivided whole. Heaven, however, divides it into its components.

Israel fought a war of seven years to conquer the Land. The inhabitants fought fiercely for their lives; we had been commanded: *Do not let a single soul live* (Devarim 20:16). Not a Jew fell in warfare. Hashem destroyed the enemy, as He had promised: *And Hashem your G-d will give them up before you and disturb them with a great disturbance until they are annihilated. And He will give their kings into your hand and you will destroy their name beneath the heavens. Not a man will stand up before you, until you annihilate them* (Devarim 7:23-24).

Thus it was throughout the seven years, with but a single exception. In the battle for Ai a number of Israelites fell. This was a sign that the Holy One was not with them: *And Yehoshua tore his clothes and fell to the ground, on his face, before the Ark of Hashem, until nightfall. He and the elders of Israel put dust on their head. And Hashem said to Yehoshua, "Get up. Why have you fallen on your face? Israel has sinned and they have also broken My treaty, which I commanded them, and they have taken from the banned goods [of Yericho], and they also stole and lied and placed [the banned goods] among their own goods. And the Children of Israel were unable to rise before their enemies; they turned tail before their enemies because they had become accursed. Nor shall I be with you anymore, if you do not destroy the banned goods from among you"* (Yehoshua 7:10-12).

The *Akeidah* wonders why there is such a detailed description of the sin. After all there was only one case of theft, yet every particular of Achan's sin is enumerated separately. Achan, too, confessed to each detail of his crime: *And I saw in the booty a coat from Shinar [Babylon], two hundred shekel of silver, one "tongue" of gold, fifty shekel in weight, and I desired them, and I took them, and behold, they are hidden in the ground* (Yehoshua 7:21). Each stage is viewed as a sin in itself: the seeing, the desiring, the taking, the hiding. This intensifies and multiplies the sin.

The Holy One, before Whom nothing is hidden, judges each stage of the sin independently. When the *Kuzari* says, "Fortunate is he whose sins are numbered," he means that his sins are not composed of stage upon stage (*Mayanei HaChaim* II:263).

❧ Deep Corruption May Be Hidden Within a Minor Sin

The Alter of Slobodka dwelt on the genesis of the sin in the corruption of the soul.

Apart from the act itself, Heaven considers the corruption of the soul which gave birth to the sin. Thus, a minor deed may reflect a terrible blemish. That is why the language used by Heaven is completely different from ours.

The prophet Yechezkel praises the righteous man, the *tzaddik* who *did not lift up his eyes to the idols of the house of Israel and did not defile his neighbor's wife and did not approach a woman in her menses* (Yechezkel 18:6). These are very major sins, ones for which one is required to give up his life rather than transgress. Is the righteous man to be praised for avoiding them? They are abominations. The *tzaddik* is one who raises himself aloft in the levels of Torah, service to Hashem, and acts of kindness to his fellowmen, not one who does not defile himself in the nether abyss!

Chazal, however, explain that he refers to not walking overly erect, lifting his head in arrogance, for "whoever is full of pride is like one who worships idols" (*Sotah* 4b).

He *did not defile his neighbor's wife*, refers to not encroaching upon another's trade. When you steal a man's livelihood, you invade his life and trample his rights. Stealing his wife is a metaphor for this invasion.

He *did not approach a woman in her menses*, means he did not take from the community charity chest. Whoever receives communal charity is not stealing from another, nor does he encroach upon another's rights. Yet *Rashi* categorizes it as a shameful act for a proper person. It is comparable to approaching a woman in her impurity. Although she is not the wife of another, she has been placed at a distance during the duration of her impurity (see *Sanhedrin* 81a).

Such is the language of Heaven. A man walks in stiff-backed pride and in Heaven this is viewed as idol worship. He encroaches upon another's trade and Heaven compares this to the theft of another's wife.

Ought we not to stand in awe at the depth of judgment? (*Or HaTzafun* II).

⇜ The Demand for Perfection

R' Yechezkel Levenstein pondered the severity of Heavenly justice. Is not the Holy One full of compassion? Does He not benefit man abundantly? Why, then, does He not temper His justice? Why does He make such a scrupulous accounting, down to the last hairsbreadth?

But that exactness in punishment, in truth, stems from the Holy One's compassion, explains R' Yechezkel. Shlomo says, *And the spirit shall return to Elokim Who gave it* (*Koheles* 12:7). And *Midrash* comments:

> Return it [the spirit] in the condition in which He gave it to you. Imagine a king who distributed royal raiment to his servants. The clever ones among them folded them and put them in a chest. The foolish ones among them, however, went and worked in them. Some time passed

and the king asked for his clothing back. The clever ones returned the garments cleaned and pressed; the fools returned them filthy. The king rejoiced in the clever ones and was angry with the fools. Of the clever ones he said, "Let their clothes be put in their storage rooms and let them go home in peace." Of the fools he said, "Let their clothes be given to the laundryman and let them be bound in prison" (*Yalkut Shimoni* to *Koheles* 12:7).

This *Midrash* explains a man's obligations in this world. Man is granted a soul, "that part of Hashem from on high." It is given to him for safekeeping, like the royal raiment given to the king's servants. And it is his duty to return it untainted, just as it was given to him. If it receives any blemish or stain whatsoever, he is held accountable. That is why Heavenly judgment is so exacting. It is intended to remove even the slightest blemish in order to allow the soul to return in purity.

❄ ❄ ❄

With this in mind we can explain another *Midrash*:

I have seen all the deeds done under the sun and all is vanity and a breaking of the spirit (*Koheles* 1:14). R' Aba ben Kahana said: "Like an old man sitting at a crossroads with two paths before him who warns the passersby. One path begins smoothly, but ends in thorns. The other begins with thorns, and ends smoothly" (*Koheles Rabbah* 1:14).

This description fits the state of man in this world. Man can only earn passage to the next world if he first walks the path of thorns. For we do not place the "royal raiment" which we received in a "chest." No! We are like "the fools among them" who "went and worked in them." Man is comprised of body and soul. Whatever is sweet to the body is like thorns to the soul. Sin dulls the heart and dims the light of the spirit. The solution? Let the clothes be given to the cleaner. That cleaning is suffering and punishment.

Yaakov chose, from the beginning, the path of thorns. Before he was born, in his mother's womb, he suffered from his brother Esav and afterwards from Lavan, his father-in-law. Later, there was the defilement of Dinah and the disappearance of Yosef. The chosen one of our forefathers summed up his life: *Few and evil have been the days of the years of my life* (*Bereishis* 47:9). This suffering was the preparation for the smooth and level part of the road, preparation for the ultimate perfection described by *Chazal*: "Our forefather Yaakov did not die" (*Taanis* 5b).

Each one of us can test his path in life to see whether it is correct or not. If the road is an easy one, it is an indication that it is not the true one. For if the going is smooth at first, the end of the road will be a thorny one.

Besides the image of the old man at the crossroads, the *Midrash* furnishes another image, that of an astrologer:

> who sits by the harbor and warns the passersby and says to them, "This kind of merchandise goes well in that place, and this kind of merchandise goes well in this place." Should men not thank him? So they should thank Shlomo who said, *I have seen all the deeds under the sun and all are vain and a breaking of the spirit* (*Koheles Rabbah* 1:14).

Shlomo warns us that anything that takes place "under the sun," anything which belongs to the material world of the body is not "desired goods" as far as the World-to-Come is concerned. Whoever carries those things there will find that he has toiled in vain and traveled for nothing. The only desired goods in the World to Come are those which are "higher than the sun," i.e., Torah, *teshuvah*, and good deeds, for these have relevance to the soul and not the body.

Heaven seeks but one thing — a soul as pure as it was when it was given to man. All that is "higher than the sun" helps the soul retain its purity and cleanse it of stains that have fallen upon it. That which is "under the sun," drags the soul down into the mud and sullies it. Even the light-hearted talk between a husband and wife is repeated to a man on his day of judgment (*Chagigah* 5b). Even the lightest of talk can cause a crease in the soul's royal raiment.

It is not an easy task. "They came to the conclusion, once and for all, that it would have been better had man not been created. But, now, that he has been created, he should examine his deeds with careful scrutiny" (*Eruvin* 13b). Before he was created, the royal clothing was new and sparkling. Now that he has been created and dirtied the royal raiment, he must give it to be laundered before he returns it to the king. *Man is born for toil* (*Iyov* 5:7); this is his labor. And if he chooses not to toil by way of *teshuvah* and good deeds, then the toil will come upon him in the form of punishment and afflictions, the path of thorns which precedes the level smooth road.

(*Or Yechezkel, Midos* 259-261)

⊷§ The Severity of the Judgment Grows in Proportion to the Greatness of the Man

R' Leib Chasman, the *mashgiach* of Chevron, described the nature of the judgment on the greatest of men.

Chazal say that the Holy One measures *tzaddikim* with a measuring rod of fire graduated down to hairsbreadths (*Bava Kamma* 50a). Why should *tzaddikim* be judged more severely? Especially since that very same *Gemara* notes that the Holy One does not overlook one's sins. Why, then, is the depth of judgment stressed for the righteous, in particular?

The *Chovos HaLevavos* writes that the expectations of a man are relative to his awareness. The more elevated a man is, the more he can grasp, the greater the demand that he conduct himself in accordance with his understanding. Thus, there are specific sacrifices for a leader who sins. Because of his loftier conception of the world, his punishment is more severe.

There is a world of difference between those who perform the *mitzvos* in an off-hand manner, of whom it is said, *And your fear of Me is a commandment of men which has been learned* (*Yesha-yahu* 29:13), and those who attain the level of *I have placed Hashem before me always* (*Tehillim* 16:8). To the latter, the Torah is always that *which I command you this day* (*Devarim* 6:6) — i.e., the laws are like edicts issued that very day.

For the righteous, each deed flows from a deep awareness; for others it is a matter of habit. And there is a difference, too, in the nature of the sins of both groups. The righteous transgress, despite their awareness, and the sin effects the very foundations of their soul. But for the former, even a sin is a matter of routine; it is a superficial act which does not make a deep impression on their dulled senses.

Chazal point out that idol worshipers were once devoted in their service to their gods. If they slaughtered an animal, they thought of it as a sacrifice. Consequently, a Jew was forbidden to make any use of the carcass. But later, they merely worshiped idols as customs that were passed down from their forefathers (see *Chulin* 13b). Even their sins were habitual and external in nature only.

In this light, we cannot speak of a "small sin," when we refer to Heavenly judgment. If we have some slight appreciation of the greatness of Hashem, if we can envision something of our obligation to serve Him, of the gratitude we owe Him, how can we imagine that a sin will be forgiven and that there is a possibility of atonement? The sin is an act of rebellion against the Holy One, Whose greatness is without bounds.

Adam understood this. He committed a single sin. As a result, he was banished from *Gan Eden*, death was decreed for him and his children for all the generations to come, the earth was cursed to produce thorns and thistles, and man was cursed to earn his sustenance by the sweat of his brow. Despite this, the Holy One informed him: "Just as you stood before Me in judgment this day [Rosh Hashanah], so your children will stand before Me in the future and emerge blameless." Even Adam's fasting and tormenting himself for one hundred and thirty years after sinning was a "kindness" compared to the dreadful sin (*Eruvin* 18b).

The fool does not feel. He is unaware of what sin is or before Whom he has sinned. His sin is a superficial act; his revolt against Heaven is superficial; and his punishment is superficial. But from the righteous, whose grasp is greater, more is demanded and the greater is their punishment.

(Or Yahel I)

⊷§ The Demand Grows in Proportion to the Awareness of the Sin

R' Aharon Kotler, *Rosh Yeshivah* of Kletzk and Lakewood emphasized the greater strictness towards *tzaddikim* from a different point of view. Not only do *tzaddikim* have a greater conception of the loftiness of the Creator and the obligation of humility before Him, they also have a better understanding of the light which a *mitzvah* brings with it and of the destructiveness of sin.

> When R' Shimon ben Gamliel and R' Yishmael [the *Kohen HaGadol*] came, [the Romans] decreed that they be slain. R' Yishmael cried, and R' Shimon said, "Young scholar, in two steps you will be placed in the laps of the *tzaddikim* and you cry?" [R' Yishmael] replied, "I weep because we are to be killed like murderers and those who desecrate the *Shabbos*." He said to him, "Perhaps you were sitting at a meal, or sleeping, and a woman came to ask concerning her menstrual cycle and your servant told her that you were sleeping. Of this the Torah says, *If you torment [the widow or orphan], I will slay you by the sword* (*Shemos* 22:22-23). Others say that R' Shimon ben Gamliel wept and R' Yishmael answered him in this fashion (*Semachos*, ch. 8).

Imagine that for such "torment" he was worthy of being slain. How can we understand this?

It is written: *Who knows the strength of Your anger? And as is Your fear so is Your wrath.* (*Tehillim* 90:11). *Who knows the strength of Your anger* — who knows the force of Hashem's aspect of justice? But we do have a guide: the aspect of justice is *as Your fear*. Just as there is no limit to the fear of Hashem — *Chazal* say that the angels stand trembling before Him until rivers of boiling sweat run from them (*Chagigah* 13b) — in such measure should there be anger for trespassing His will.

If, then, we cannot conceive the fear of the Holy One, perhaps our sins are granted a degree of absolution; perhaps Heavenly judgment does not penetrate as deeply where we are involved.

The *Beis HaLevi*, however, refutes this conclusion. Let us say a man gives a package to another for safekeeping and says that it contains inexpensive ornamental jewelry. If the guardian is negligent and loses the package, he is liable only for the value of the inexpensive jewelry, even if the package in reality contained diamonds. The guardian only accepted responsibility for inexpensive jewelry and nothing more.

However, if the guardian were to take the package and cast it into the sea, he would be required to pay for diamonds. He would not be able to say that he only wanted to get rid of a less valuable object, because he had no right to cause damage even to an inexpensive package (See *Bava Kamma* 62a).

Let us apply these *halachos* to our topic. True, we have hardly any grasp of Hashem's greatness and awe. But if we cause damage with our own hands, if we intentionally commit a sin, then we are punished with all the severity appropriate to the sin. We shall not be able to say in response that we had no idea of the extent of the judgment. For we will be told, "Was what you did permitted in the light of your grasp of things? Since even for you this is a sin, you are to be indicted as if you were a prophet or an angel."

Besides this aspect of "damaging with one's own hands," there is the matter of carelessness. Here we speak of sins committed through inattentiveness. For such sins Heaven judges us in terms of "what we thought the package contained." It is common for us simple souls to consider all of our activity as of small note. After all, what can we accomplish in the upper worlds with our actions?

This is, however, not true! Whoever ponders the issue more deeply knows that *Hashem established the earth in wisdom, founded the heaven in understanding* (*Mishlei* 3:19). We cannot contemplate how much wisdom is latent in the structure of each grain of sand. But beyond that there is a higher wisdom expressed in the conjunction of the material world and that of the spirit: "There is not a blade of grass over which a spirit does not stand and smite it and say, 'Grow!' " (*Bereishis Rabbah* 10:6). If this is true for the most minute creation, how much more so does it apply to man who does not bruise his finger unless it has been proclaimed from on high (*Chullin* 7b). The Torah is the root of all existence and man can "add to the force of the heavenly entourage" (*Zohar* I:4) or "weaken the force of the heavenly entourage" (*Chullin* 7b).

Chazal say, "Man was created alone so that each man might say, 'For me was the world created'" (*Sanhedrin* 38a). Furthermore, we are told, "The world was created only to serve the righteous man" (*Shabbos* 30b). The creation of the entire world was worthwhile to serve a single perfect man. This shows us how high man's actions reach. The more man is aware of the importance of his deeds, the greater is the charge against him for the carelessness of his acts.

(*Mishnas R' Aharon* II)

◆§ Conclusion

A ll that we have said is contained in essence in the words of R' Chaim Volozhin:

> There are three distinct aspects of Divine judgment. Each aspect of the sin is judged individually: A man is told even of the light-hearted talk between himself and his wife in the hour of his judgment, as it says (*Amos* 4:13), "*He tells a man what he has said*" (*Chagigah* 5b).

A man does not pay attention to what comes forth from his lips. He thinks to himself, what difference does a light jest or an obscenity make? He does not realize that it touches his soul. He has no idea how far his talk reaches. All that happens in the upper worlds is a result of human action, speech and behavior. That is the meaning of the verse, *And man became a living being* (*Bereishis* 2:7) — he is the soul and life-force of all the worlds and all are influenced by his actions.

[When the prophet says,] *"He tells a man what he has said,"* he means that the Holy One reveals to him what effect his words have had, how many worlds he has destroyed with a light jest.

When the verse says, *He perceives* (הַמֵּבִין אֶל) *all of their deeds* (*Tehillim* 33:15), it means not only that the Holy One understands their deeds but that he knows until what point (אֶל מַה) they have reached — i.e., how much destruction they have caused.

The punishment is proportional to the fault and the fault is judged in terms of the greatness of the soul. That is the second aspect of Divine judgment. The loftier the soul, the more it is rooted in the higher worlds, the farther do the effects of the sin reach. There is a difference between one who dirties the courtyard of a king and one who dirties his palace, between one who dirties the king's throne and one who soils his raiment.

Thus, although two men may commit the same sin, their punishment will not be identical. Each is to be judged in terms of his own soul.

❀ ❀ ❀

We can better understand the third aspect of Divine judgment with a military metaphor. When a private is remiss and does not do his duty, he puts himself in danger, but he does not cause harm to the army as a whole. But, if a brigade commander is negligent, he may cause the loss of his entire brigade. And if the commanding general is careless, he may cause the destruction of his entire army.

Similarly, *Chazal* have said, "Whoever is able to protest against [the improper acts of] the members of his household, and does not do so, will be punished for the deeds of the members of his household. Whoever is able to protest against [the improper acts of] the members of his town, and does not do so, will be punished for the deeds of the members of his town. Whoever is able to protest against [the improper acts of] the whole world, and does not do so, will be punished for the deeds of the entire world" (*Shabbos* 54b).

The principle is this: A man is judged by the extent of the damage and destruction caused by his sins both in our world and in the upper worlds.

(From his discourse for Rosh Hashanah)

Part Three:
Reflections by the Masters of Mussar

◆§ You Have Upset My Entire Plan

R' NOSSON TZVI FINKEL (THE ALTER OF SLOBODKA)

When Hashem created woman, he thought, "I shall not create her from the head so that she will not be full of pride; nor from the eye so that she will not be inquisitive; nor from the ear so that she might not be an eavesdropper, but rather from a hidden part of man." And with the creation of each of her limbs, He said, "Be a modest woman." Despite this — You have upset My entire plan (Mishlei 1:25). [He said,] "I did not create her from the head, and yet she is full of pride; as it is said, And they [the daughters of Jerusalem] walked with outstretched necks (Yeshayahu 3:16); nor from the eye, and yet she is inquisitive, as it is said, and they stared about (ibid.); nor from the ear, and yet she eavesdrops, as it is said, And Sarah was listening at the entrance of the tent (Bereishis 18:10).   *(Bereishis Rabbah 18:2)*

If we reflect upon the complaint against Sarah for listening at the tent's opening, we cannot help but notice that her indiscretion was exceptionally minor. She overheard the angels deliver a prophetic message, on a matter that touched her — i.e., that she was to give birth to a son. Nor had she intended to eavesdrop, for the ear is an organ that man does not control. And even after Sarah was criticized, we still find that she possessed a greater measure of prophecy than Avraham (*Rashi* on *Bereishis* 21:12).

Though Sarah's sin was exceptionally minor, the Holy One, Who examines the innermost workings of man's mind, compared it to the sin of the daughters of Zion who, by walking with "outstretched necks" and "staring eyes," caused the young men of Israel to fall into sin and thereby brought about the Destruction of the Temple. Because of that act, Sarah is called an eavesdropper and made an example of the charge against woman in general: *You have upset My entire plan*. How frightening are the depths of Heavenly judgment. How great is the destructive force of sin! For the lightest of sins is equal in weight to the most serious.

But the other side of the coin is no less overwhelming. The daughters of Zion brought the young men of Israel to sin because of their pride. And when the prophet warned them about the forthcoming Destruction, they said, *Let Him quickly hurry and do His deed, that we might see* (*Yeshayahu* 5:19). *Chazal* portray each as saying, "An enemy officer will see me and take me to wife" (*Yalkut Shimoni: Yeshayahu* 499). They welcomed the Destruction. Yet the complaint directed at them is exactly the same as the one against Sarah — *You have upset My entire plan* — and so, too, is the implicit demand made of them: "Why did you not rise to the level of the perfect man?"

That question will be posed to each human being. He will be asked (*Tanna D'vei Eliyahu* 25), "Why did your deeds not reach the level of Your forefathers, Avraham, Yitzchak, and Yaakov?"

(*Or HaTzafun* I *Vatifre'u chol atzasi*)

◄§ The Effect of Sin

R' SIMCHAH ZISSEL (THE ALTER OF KELM)

Behold how sin deadens a person. Before Adam sinned, the Holy One spoke to him while he was naked. But after he transgressed the mild prohibition which had been placed upon him, everything changed (see *Shabbos* 55b). Even after one hundred and thirty years of bitter repentance (*Eruvin* 18b); even twenty generations later, after Avraham had withstood all of Hashem's trials and been found to be true of heart (Satan himself testified that Avraham never questioned Hashem's actions (*Bava Basra* 15b); Avraham still could not hear Hashem speak even when fully clothed, until he had circumcised himself (*Rashi* on *Bereishis* 17:1). Transgression of a single mild prohibition had this great effect. How great then, is the effect of many sins, let alone many serious sins?

The daughters of Lot meant well in wanting offspring from their father. Their deed was done for the sake of Heaven. They thought that mankind had been destroyed, just as it had been wiped out in the age of the Flood (*Rashi* on *Bereishis* 19:31). And since a descendant of Noach is permitted to join with his daughter (*Sanhedrin* 58b), they hoped to repopulate the world through their father. Yet, when all is said and done, since a daughter was to be forbidden to her father in the future, after the giving of the Torah, Ammon and Moav are seen as improperly conceived and are forbidden to enter the assembly of Israel forever. The sin was mild; the consequences overwhelming.

(*Chochmah U'Mussar* I:188)

⇜ Behold the Righteous Man Shall Be Paid Upon the Earth

R' NOSSON TZVI FINKEL (THE ALTER OF SLOBODKA)

Noach was a righteous man, whole in his generations; Noach walked with Elokim (Bereishis 6:9). Each step Noach took was with Hashem.

> These are the offspring of Noach, Noach...(Bereishis 5:9): As his name (נֹחַ) indicates, he was pleasing (וְנִיחָא) to himself, he was pleasing to the world; he was pleasing to fathers, he was pleasing to sons; he was pleasing to those who live above in the heavens and to those who live below on earth; he was pleasing in this world, he was pleasing in the next. These are the offspring of Noach: This is what is meant by the verse, the fruit of the righteous man is a living tree (Mishlei 11:30) — the offspring of a righteous man are the mitzvos he performs and his good deeds (Bereishis Rabbah 30:5-6).

Even the angels, who had been critical of the creation of man, ceased finding fault when they saw Noach (Rashi on Bereishis Rabbah 30:5).

Hashem tests the righteous man (Tehillim 11:5). For twelve months Noach walked in the ways of the Creator. For just as it is said of the Creator, The eyes of all look towards You, and You give them their food in its proper time (Tehillim 145:15), so Noach supplied all the needs of the creatures in the Ark:

> "It was difficult for us in the Ark," said Shem, Noach's son, to Eliezer, the servant of Avraham. "Those creatures who are accustomed to eat by day, we fed by day. Those who eat at night, we fed at night" (Sanhedrin 108b).

> In the twelve months in the Ark, Noach did not sleep

a wink, day or night. He was busy feeding the animals which were there with him. (*Tanchuma, Noach* 9).

And his sufferings grew from day to day. For, as the *Beis HaLevi* has noted, when a man is beaten by one blow after another, even when they are of equal intensity, he feels each successive blow more acutely than the previous one. The pain is cumulative; "the heat at the end of the summer is harder to bear than all of the summer."

At the end of those twelve months, when Noach was leaving the Ark, the lion struck him, wounding him in such as way as to render him unfit to offer up a sacrifice. His son Shem brought the sacrifice in his stead (*Bereishis Rabbah* 30:6). The lion attacked Noach because he had once been late in feeding him. This shows us what demands are made of us and what damage a small failing can cause.

The Torah itself tells us of Noach's righteousness. Noach elevated himself to the level of imitating Hashem, so to speak, in His role as sustainer of all the living — feeding tender branches to the elephants and [grass] to the ostriches, all the while not sleeping at all. Finally, when that twelve-month period drew to a close and "he was spitting up blood from the cold," he was late once in feeding the lion. With that, the lion lost his awe of man. No longer did the verse, *The fear and terror of you will rest on all the beasts of the earth* (*Bereishis* 9:2), apply to Noach. The lion then saw him as an animal (see *Shabbos* 151b). He was struck and blemished, and thereby rendered unfit to offer up a sacrifice — a punishment both to the body and soul. On this the *Midrash* (*Tanchuma, Noach* 9) comments: "Of him [Noach] it is said, *Behold! The righteous man shall be paid upon the earth*" (*Mishlei* 11:31).

Of him the *Midrash* says, "The righteous man is punished in this world." How far reaching is the judgment!

(*Or HaTzafun* I, *Dakus HaTeviah*)

◄§ Putting Effort Into a Mitzvah

R' DOV MEIR RUBMAN

*A*nd Shem and Yefes took the garment and put it on the shoulders of both of them (Bereishis 9:23). Rashi notes that the first verb — took — is in the singular, he took (וַיִּקַּח), not the plural, they took (וַיִּקְחוּ). This shows that Shem made a greater effort than did Yefes (Rashi on Bereishis 9:23).

It is difficult to see the greater effort in Shem's performance of the *mitzvah*. Both took the garment; both placed it on their shoulders; both walked with their heads averted. But the Torah indicates that Shem devoted more effort.

And because of Shem's greater effort, "his children [Israel] were destined to gain the *talis* of *tzitzis*" (Rashi ibid.). And the *mitzvah* of *tzitzis* is considered equal to all the *mitzvos* combined (Menachos 43b).

Noach blessed him: *Blessed is Hashem, the G-d of Shem* (Bereishis 9:26) — the Divine Presence will rest upon his descendants, Israel. But the Divine Presence did not rest on the second Temple, which was built by Cyrus, who was descended from Yefes (Rashi on Bereishis 9:27).

Yefes performed precisely the same *mitzvah* with but a trifle less effort than Shem. And the consequence: he did not gain for his descendants the *mitzvos* or the Land of Israel. Nor does the Divine Presence rest upon his descendants.

> Ben Hai Hai said to Hillel, . . . *And you will return and see [the difference] between the righteous man and the evildoer, between one who serves Elokim and one who does not serve Him* (Malachi 3:18). . . . Hillel said to him, "The one who serves *Elokim* and the one who does not are both fully righteous men. But one cannot compare the man who has reviewed his learning one hundred times to the man who has done so one hundred and one times."

"And because of that single time, he is said not to serve *Elokim?*" said Bar Hai Hai.

"Yes," said Hillel. "Go to the market where drivers hire out their donkeys. They take a *zuz* for a trip of ten parasangs, but two *zuz* for a distance of eleven parasangs" (*Chagigah* 9b).

One more review, a bit more effort — and already he cannot be compared to his friend who did not make the extra effort. They are totally different.

(*Zichron Meir* 12)

৽§ The Two Words Which Wiped Away Forty-Eight Years

R' YEHUDAH LEIB CHASMAN

Sarah wished to bring a rival into her home, hoping thereby, that she would be rewarded with the birth of children — *Perhaps I will build from her* (*Bereishis* 16:2 and *Rashi* ad loc.). Sarah persuaded Hagar to agree (*Bereishis Rabbah* 45:3). So great was Sarah's deed and so difficult that in its merit, nature was changed and a miracle occurred.

Hagar turned on her mistress and publicly slandered her with a vile charge: "Sarah is a hypocrite; she is not what she appears to be. She shows herself as a righteous woman but she is not. . ." (*Rashi* on *Bereishis* 16:4). Sarah judged her as deserving a punishment — a judgment based on the Divine Inspiration. *And Avraham listened to the voice of Sarah* (*Bereishis* 16:2) — to the voice of Divine Inspiration within her (*Bereishis Rabbah*).

And an angel agreed that Hagar should be punished: *Return to your mistress and let yourself suffer under her hands* (*Bereishis* 16:9).

Because Avraham had not been quick to react to Hagar's slander of her mistress, Sarah declared that Heaven should judge between herself and her husband (*Bereishis* 16:5). *Chazal* comment:

> Whoever takes another before the [Heavenly] court is punished first. For it is said: *And Sarah said, "May the theft [I have suffered] be on you"* (*Bereishis* 16:5), and it is written: *And Avraham came to lament for Sarah and weep for her* (*Bereishis* 23:2). This is so if there are courts on earth (*Bava Kamma* 93a).

And *Tosafos* explains that "courts on earth" refers to that of Shem which was in existence in Sarah's day.

Sarah was not faulted for the charge she brought against Avraham, or for the way in which she expressed herself. But she was criticized by *Chazal* for not taking him before a human court. Yet, why should she have? Her own claim, *May the theft... be on you*, should have been enough to induce Avraham to agree to her position.

By demanding that they appear before the Heavenly court, Sarah expressed her absolute confidence in the justice of her claim. But as long as a human court — which can clarify the truth — exists, one is forbidden to be so certain of himself. This is so, even when one is acting on the basis of Divine Inspiration, which Sarah possessed in greater measure than Avraham (*Rashi* on *Bereishis* 21:12). Even though an angel agreed with her, even though she was fully justified, her great act of charity was thrown in her face!

Sarah was at fault and she was punished. She did not live to see her only son return from the *Akeidah*. Though the act of offering up Yitzchak was destined to protect Israel throughout the generations, it did not serve to protect Yitzchak's own mother: *And Avraham came to lament for Sarah and weep for her* (*Bereishis* 23:2).

The *Gemara* cites that verse with reference to punishment for demanding a hearing before Heaven. And the *Maharsha* explains that were it not for Sarah's demand for a Heavenly judgment, she would have outlived Avraham by ten years. Because she spoke two words (חֲמָסִי עָלֶיךָ) and exhibited a minor failing, she forfeited forty-eight additional years of holiness and purity, of *mitzvos* and good deeds. For the years of Sarah's life were *all equally good*.

(*Or Yahel* III: *Vayera*)

✦§ The Hair Stands on End

R' BEN ZION BRUK

> *And Avraham said, "Hashem Elokim, what will You give me? (Bereishis 15:2). Said the Holy One, "Avraham went into battle, and I made him monarch over sixteen kings. I brought the prisoners back to him. He thought that, perhaps, that was his reward and I said to him, 'Have no fear Avraham, your reward is very great.' Should he not have given praise? But what did he say? 'Hashem Elokim, what will You give me?' Man's foolishness twists his path (Mishlei 19:3).* (*Aggados Bereishis 65*)

Your hair stands on end when you read this. To whom are *Chazal* applying this verse of *Mishlei?* To Avraham. Avraham who was willing to be martyred in the fiery oven; Avraham who successfully passed every test to which he was put. The *Rambam* even understands the verse: *And he [Avraham] believed in Hashem and he considered it as righteousness (Bereishis 15:6)*, to mean that Avraham [not Hashem] thought that Hashem was acting righteously — i.e., rewarding him beyond his deserts in promising him a son.

Nevertheless, *Chazal* felt that there was something greatly amiss in Avraham's question, *What will You give me*, for Avraham stressed what he was lacking rather than what he had been given.

He is criticized though he was lacking a great deal, for he who lacks sons is as one dead and destroyed (*Bereishis Rabbah* 45:3).

And I am childless (*Bereishis* 15:3). Avraham said to the Holy One, "Master of the Universe, What pleasure do I have from all that You have given me when You have not granted me children?" (*Aggadas Bereishis* 37). Was he asking for children for his own sake? No! He wished to establish the nation Israel and proclaim Hashem's name in the world — *That he might command his sons and his household after him so that they would guard Hashem's path by doing righteousness and justice* (*Bereishis* 18:19).

Nevertheless, he was judged severely.

(*Hegionei Mussar, Vayigash*)

✎§ By What Shall I Know

R' NOSSON TZVI FINKEL (THE ALTER OF SLOBODKA)

Avraham was the first of the believers. He was the first to call the Holy One, Master (*Berachos* 7a). He was tested in ten trials and his heart was found faithful (*Nechemiah* 9:8). Of him, it is said: *And he believed in Hashem* (*Bereishis* 15:6). When Moshe *Rabbeinu* said: *They will not believe me* (*Shemos* 4:1), the Holy One said to him, "They are believers [and] the children of believers; Believers — as it is written, *And the nation believed* (*Shemos* 4:31); the children of believers — as it is written, *And he (Avraham) believed in Hashem* (*Bereishis* 15:6; see *Shabbos* 97a).

Nevertheless, *Chazal* have said, "Why was Avraham punished and his children enslaved to Egypt for two hundred and ten years? Because he questioned the ways of the Holy One, by asking, 'By what shall I know that I will inherit it" (*Nedarim* 32a)?

Elsewhere *Chazal* have interpreted Avraham's question, "By what shall I know," as an explanation of Avraham's concern as to Israel's worthiness to gain the land. The Holy One answered that Israel would receive the land by virtue of the sacrifices (*Taanis* 27b). Because of Avraham's elevated spiritual level and lofty mind, his use of an expression which might be understood as a request to Hashem to furnish proof for His promise was held against him in Heaven. The comment of the *Midrash* (*Tanchuma, Kedoshim* 13) on this incident is: Woe to the man who says something and does not know how to say it properly. Because Avraham said, "By what shall I know," he was told, *Know [they] will be strangers in a land not their own for four hundred years* (*Bereishis* 15:13). For this slightly ambiguous remark, Avraham's descendants were enslaved for generations to the lowly Egyptians, descendants of Canaan, who was cursed to be *a slave of slaves* (*Bereishis* 9:25). That servitude was to coarsen the Children of Israel, to such an extent, that the angels on high would argue, "How are these — Israel — different from these — the Egyptians" (*Mechilta, Beshalach*)?

They were to make bricks, build buildings, and work in the fields. They were to endure backbreaking physical labor and descend to the forty-ninth level of impurity of the soul. And all this for such a slight, almost unnoticeable failing, a quickly passing taint on the brightly shining faith of the father of believers.

Only the Holy One, Himself, in His glory could bring Israel out of their exile — not an angel nor a seraph nor a messenger. For the cause of that bitter, terrible exile was a fault so slight that only the Holy One Himself, Who examines man's innermost thoughts, could determine when the time had come to correct it. Only through the revelation of the Holy One Himself, in all His Glory, could Israel repair that almost imperceivable fault hidden by the question, "By what shall I know?"

(*Or HaTzafun* I, *Avdus V'Cherus*)

☙ It Is a Greater Mitzvah
If He Does It,
Rather than His Agent

R' NOSSON FINKEL (THE ALTER OF SLOBODKA)

Our forefather Avraham sat at the opening of his tent looking for guests on the third day after his circumcision, tightening and loosening his bandage. Hashem caused the sun to shine at its full strength so that no one could endure its heat. Yet, despite the heat and the pain, Avraham sought guests (*Bava Metzia* 86b). Even the appearance of the Divine Presence did not deter Avraham.

Finally, the Holy One sent three angels in the guise of Arabs, worshipers of the very dust of their feet. And he, Avraham, old and in pain though he was, ran to them in the midday heat, bowed down before them and begged them to come into the shadow of his tent. He ran to the cattle to slaughter three oxen and offer them each an ox tongue in mustard. He told Sarah to hurry and bake cakes for them. There was one single detail in which he did not involve himself personally. He did not supply the water himself, probably because he was busy preparing their meal: *Let a little water be brought and wash your feet* (*Bereishis* 18:4). And yet:

> R' Yehudah said in the name of Rav: Whatever Avraham himself did for the angels, the Holy One did for [Avraham's] descendants. And whatever Avraham did for them by proxy, Hashem did for his children by proxy.
>
> *And Avraham ran to the cattle* (*Bereishis* 18:7); *And a wind went forth from Hashem and brought quails from the sea* (*Bamidbar* 11:31).
>
> *And he took butter and milk* (*Bereishis* 18:18); *Behold I shall rain down bread for you from the heavens* (*Shemos* 16:4).

And he stood attendance upon them under the tree (*Bereishis* 18:8); *Behold I shall stand before you on the rock* (*Shemos* 17:6).

And Avraham accompanied them to send them off (*Bereishis* 18:16); *And Hashem went before them by day*. . . (*Shemos* 13:21).

[And by contrast, what Avraham did not do himself, Hashem did through an emissary.] *Let a little water be taken* (*Bereishis* 18:4); *And you [Moshe] will smite the rock and water will come forth* (*Shemos* 17:6).

(*Bava Metzia* 86b)

And Hashem went before them by day. Israel merited being accompanied by Hashem because Avraham himself accompanied the angels and saw them off. But is there, indeed, such a great distinction between the presence of Hashem's proxy and that of Himself which Israel would have attained had Avraham not delegated the task of accompanying his guests to Ishmael or Eliezer? Moshe tells us that there is a difference: *If Your presence* [literally *face*] *does not go with us, do not take us up from here* (*Shemos* 33:15). It would have been preferable for Israel to remain forever in the dry, inhospitable wilderness, and forego the Promised Land, if Hashem Himself would continue to accompany them and not an angel.

Had Avraham himself given the water to the angels, the Holy One would Himself have given water and the tragedy at the Waters of Strife (*mei m'rivah*) would not have occurred. Moshe would have led Israel into the Land; the *Beis Hamikdash* would not have been destroyed and we would not have gone into exile (*Sotah* 14). Because Avraham neglected a single, minor detail in his great act of kindness, we lost all this.

(*Or HaTzafun* I, *Hada'as Sheb'ma'aseh*)

◄§ Why Is the Wholly Burnt Animal Sacrificed

R' NOSSON TZVI FINKEL (THE ALTER OF SLOBODKA)

Teach us, our master, why was the olah [the wholly burnt offering] sacrificed. . .? R' Shimon bar Yochai answered, "For thoughts of the heart, as it is said: And it was when the days of banqueting had come full circle, Iyov would invite them and he would rise early and offer up wholly burnt sacrifices equal to the number of his children. For Iyov said, 'Perhaps my children have sinned and expressed themselves unfittingly in their hearts towards Hashem.' So did Iyov do all the days (Iyov 1:5). We find that Avraham [was troubled and] thought about Divine justice. What did he say to himself? 'Probably I have received my entire reward in this world. The Holy One aided me against the four kings and saved me from the fiery furnace. I have already received my reward and have no further reward.' [Thereupon], the Holy One said to him, 'Because you have questioned My deeds, you must sacrifice an olah, Take your son, your only one and offer him up as an olah'" (Bereishis 22:2).

(Tanchuma, Lech Lecha)

Amazing! Avraham went into the fiery furnace to sanctify the name of Hashem. In the war against the four kings, he praised Hashem and won for him dominion over the earth and the heavens (*Sotah* 4b). Nevertheless, he did not rest easy. He viewed himself precisely as *Chazal* said a man should: "A man should never put himself in danger, for he may not be granted a miracle from Heaven. And if a miracle does occur, something is subtracted from the sum total of his rewards" (*Taanis* 20b). And Avraham had experienced many miracles. He had thrown straw at the enemy and it had turned into arrows; earth, and it had turned into swords (*Taanis* 21a). His concern was well founded and *Chazal* praised him for it. They applied the verse, *Fortunate is the man who is constantly in fear* (*Mishlei* 28:14), to him (*Tanchuma*, *Lech Lecha* 15).

But Hashem, in His aspect of justice (*midas hadin*), took Avraham to task for this fear. Hashem saw in his heart, loyal though he was, a trace of a misconception concerning G-d's kindness, which is boundless. As a consequence, Avraham was required to bring an *olah* to atone for that thought. And what a sacrifice — his only son from Sarah, the son whom Hashem had granted him when he was one hundred years old, the son who was to be called his seed and become the foundation of the nation Israel. And that nation was to receive the Torah, enter the Holy Land, build the *Beis Hamikdash* and look forward to the End of Days! What depths does Divine justice hold! Whose mind can encompass it?

(*Or HaTzafun I, Kocho shel Hirhur*)

ᴖᴿ False Scales

R' NOSSON TZVI FINKEL (THE ALTER OF SLOBODKA)

*E*liezer, the servant of Avraham, considered proposing his daughter as a match for Yitzchak. To this, *Chazal* applied the verse, *Canaan holds scales of fraud in his hand to steal from the one who loves (Hoshea 12:8). Canaan is Eliezer. Holds scales of fraud in his hand* — Eliezer sat and evaluated his daughter to determine whether she was worthy or not. *To steal from the one who loves* —refers to one who is beloved by the world, i.e., Yitzchak (*Yalkut Shimoni* 107).

Eliezer drew and gave others to drink from his master Avraham's Torah; his features were like those of Avraham and he ruled supreme over his desires like his master (*Yalkut Shimoni* 106). Yet, because he entertained an improper thought in his soul, though he did not come to a final conclusion, much less act upon it, he is called a cheat and a robber.

(Or HaTzafun, Hanistar Sheb'nigleh)

ঙ্গ And His Hand Holds the Heel

R' NOSSON TZVI FINKEL (THE ALTER OF SLOBODKA)

When Yaakov sent Binyamin, his beloved son, down to Egypt with his brothers, he prayed for his safe return and said, "I have suffered much. When I was yet in my mother's womb Esav fought with me... Let He who said 'enough' to the heavens and earth, say 'enough' to my sufferings" (*Tanchuma Miketz* 11).

Generations later, the prophet Hoshea laments: *Hashem has a quarrel with Yehudah, and will remember Yaakov according to his ways. He will repay him as befits his actions. In the womb he grasped his brother's heel...* (*Hoshea* 12:3-4). The Holy One demands retribution from Israel for Yaakov's sin, the sin of holding onto Esav's heel when he came out of the womb. Thus, even the "sin" of an infant at birth is considered oppression which demands retribution for generations to come.

(*Or HaTzafun* I, *Omek HaDin*)

⊸§ Do Not Glory in the Morrow

R' YOSEF YOIZEL HOROWITZ (THE ALTER OF NOVARDHOK)

The Torah demands that a man be educated to perfection and not miss the mark by a hair.

Yaakov was the chosen one of the *Avos* (*Bereishis Rabbah* 76:1); the Holy One called him by His own name, *E-l* (*Megillah* 18a). He guarded the sheep of his father-in-law Lavan as carefully as he could, though he was aware of Lavan's fraudulent ways. And Lavan did indeed change the terms of their agreement ten times. Yaakov wished to clear himself from any possible suspicion in the future and have a clear proof as to which lambs were his: *My righteousness will answer for me on the morrow when it will come, on my wages before you — when it,* my righteousness, *will come* to testify on my behalf *before you* concerning my wages — *whatever is not spotted and speckled of the kids and brown of the lambs will be [considered] as stolen [goods] in my possession* (*Bereishis* 30:33).

It is on this verse that the *Midrash* comments:

> R' Yehudah bar Shimon says: "It is written: *Do not glory in the morrow* (*Mishlei* 27:1). You have said, *My righteousness will answer for me on the morrow.* Tomorrow your daughter will go forth and be violated, as it is written, *And Dinah the daughter of Leah went forth*" (*Bereishis* 34:1). (*Bereishis Rabbah* 73:9)

The *Eitz Yosef* points out that the word for violation in the story of Dinah (וַיְעַנֶּהָ; *Bereishis* 34:2) recalls the expression 'will answer for me" (וְעָנְתָה בִּי; *Bereishis* 30:33).

Because Yaakov possessed a supreme level of trust in the Holy One, his thought about the next day was deemed as lacking that same level of trust.

(*Madregos Ha'adam, Darkei Habitachon* chapter 3)

◆§ Why Did Rachel Die First?

R' YOEL KLEINERMAN OF SHINOVA

*A*nd Rachel and Leah answered and said to him (Bereishis 31:14). Why did Rachel die first? R' Yehudah said that it was because she spoke before her sister (*Bereishis Rabbah* 74:4). Whoever reads this shudders when he realizes the task incumbent upon him and the need to reach perfection.

Rachel had given up all her hope for a spiritual future and agreed that Leah should marry Yaakov, even though she knew that Yaakov preferred her, and had clearly stipulated to Lavan that he had chosen Rachel. Yet, Rachel gave Leah the signs which she and Yaakov had made up, so that Leah would not be found out and embarrassed. She should have been fearful that after Leah married Yaakov, she would be forced to marry Esav. For *Chazal* say that common folk were saying that Rivkah had two sons and Lavan had two daughters; the older daughter would marry the older son, the younger daughter the younger son. Leah had, indeed, feared this and wept copiously, so much so, that her eyelashes fell out (*Bava Basra* 123a). The Torah alludes to this when it writes, *and Leah's eyes were weak* (*Bereishis* 29:17). Now that Leah was married to Yaakov, Rachel remained for Esav. And to all this Rachel had agreed. Can there be a higher conception of perfection?

And after Rachel was married to Yaakov, it was she that became the principal homekeeper as it is written: *And he called for Rachel and Leah* (*Bereishis* 31:4).

> Rachel is mentioned first because she was the principal homekeeper. It was for her sake that Yaakov had agreed to marry into the family of Lavan. Even Leah's descendants admit that. For Boaz and his court from the tribe of Yehudah said, *Like Rachel and Leah who both built...* (*Ruth* 4:11). They put Rachel before Leah (*Rashi* on *Bereishis* 31:4).

After all this, did not Rachel have the right to speak before her sister? And for doing so is she to be viewed as having sinned greatly and punished by dying first?

We see that, despite all that Rachel had done, she must still honor Leah, her older sister, and not speak out of turn, so that Leah would not feel in any way the weight of Rachel's good deeds. And since Rachel did not, the Holy One judged her as He judges the righteous, by that fine ruler which measures even the width of a hair.

(Gevilei Esh)

~§ Thirty-three!

R' SIMCHAH ZISSEL (THE ALTER OF KELM)

It is astonishing how carefully things are weighed on the Heavenly scales of justice. The *Baal HaTurim* notes that Yaakov lived thirty-three years less than his father Yitzchak. For it is written: *An empty curse will come upon him (Mishlei 26:2).* Because he inadvertently cursed Rachel and said, *Anyone with whom you shall find your gods shall not live (Bereishis 31:32),* Yaakov lost the number of years equal to the numerical value of "live" (יחיה) — thirty-three (*Baal HaTurim on Bereishis 47:28*).

Yaakov did not know that Rachel had taken the idols. However, because it did not dawn upon him that perhaps, someone in his household had taken them, hidden them in the camel's cushion, and said, *I am in the way of women (Bereishis 31:35),* a heavy punishment — the loss of thirty-three years of life — was imposed upon him. Imagine! He was heavily punished for what was almost accidental — for failing to take into consideration such a farfetched possibility!

How shall we face the Day of Judgment, the Day of Reproof? Imagine the punishment of a man who does not consider obvious possibilities — those which occur many times a day!

(*Chochmah U'Mussar* I: *Ma'amar* 97)

◆§ Perhaps I Sullied Myself with Sin

R' SIMCHAH ZISSEL (THE ALTER OF KELM)

*L*et me briefly comment on the depth of Divine justice and the great joy which is the reward for a *mitzvah*. Even the greatest of men could not in a lifetime fully appreciate the wonderment of the joy.

Yaakov said: *I am small because of all the kindnesses and all the truth which You have done for Your servant. For I crossed the Jordan with my staff and now I have become two camps (Bereishis 32:11).*

Rashi explains: *I am small:* My stock of credit has been reduced because of the kindnesses which You have done for me. Therefore I fear lest I have sullied myself with sin, after Your promises to me, and this will cause me to be handed over to Esav. *All the truth:* The truth of what You have said. You kept all the promises You made to me. *For. . . with my staff:* I had neither silver, nor gold, nor cattle, just my staff itself.

In the previous verse, *Rashi* commented: "Yaakov said to the Holy One, 'You made two promises to me when I left my father's house in Beer Sheva. You said, *I shall keep guard over you wherever you go (Bereishis* 28:15). And in Lavan's house You said, *Return to the land of your fathers and your birthplace and I will be with you. . . (Bereishis* 32:10). It is with these two promises [in mind] that

I come before you" (*Rashi* on *Bereishis* 32:10). "I come before you" to pray "lest I have sullied myself with sin and this will cause me to be handed over to Esav."

What sin had Yaakov committed? Had he not taken his life into his hands to receive the blessing meant for his brother Esav? And he did this for the sake of the future Israel at Rivkah's direction. Rivkah had been told by Heaven that Yaakov would not be cursed (see *Onkelos* on *Bereishis* 27:13) and it was Heaven's will that Yaakov receive the blessings (*Tanchuma Toledos* 7). The *Yalkut* says that while he was walking towards his father, Yaakov wept. Most likely he feared, *Perhaps, my father will touch me* (*Bereishis* 27:12). Afterwards it was necessary that he leave home and go to Lavan's. There he worked fourteen years, including sleepless nights, to please Hashem and to establish the twelve tribes for which the Holy One had created the world. And while there, he kept the 613 *mitzvos* (*Rashi* on *Bereishis* 32:5). With what sin, then, had he sullied himself?

I think that Yaakov's major fear was hinted at in his statement, *For I crossed this Jordan with my staff and now I have become two camps* (*Bereishis* 32:11). Perhaps he felt that a taint of the desire for money had crept up upon him. For it is from this that *Chazal* learn that the righteous are more concerned with their possessions than their bodies (*Chullin* 91a). Yaakov was worried that he did not have precisely the right attitude towards money. Lot's example stood before him. Lot had become sullied by a desire for money after he became wealthy, a desire beyond that which was fitting for a man of his lofty stature. Lavan, too, had become tainted by a lust for money. Yaakov had a fear that his wealth and his living with Lavan had tainted him as well. No man can know the very fine shades of sin. Only the All-knowing — Who searches out the heart and examines the insides, the seats of feeling and thought — can know.

Yaakov did not love his sons because they were his sons, but because they were beloved by Hashem. This is evident from his treatment of Reuven. His eldest son had done something trifling. It was not a true sin. "Whoever says that Reuven sinned is mistaken," (*Shabbos* 55b). Not only did Yaakov not bless him, he took away from him the rights of the firstborn, the priesthood and the monarchy (*Onkelos* on *Bereishis* 49:3-4). Because of a single incident in which he acted hastily, Reuven was characterized as *unstable as water*, and lost all these things.

If, then, Yaakov prayed, *lest he come and smite me, mother and children* (*Bereishis* 32:12), he was praying for them not as members of his family, but as the totality of Israel. Why, then, his concern, "I am small?" It is awesome to think that if the greatest of men commits the most insignificant of sins, no promises in the world are binding.

Let us imagine the close friend of a king. The king has promised him everything. But if they become estranged, will the king honor his promises? The Holy One promises to grant benefits to those who are close to Him. But only when they are close. With but a slight fault man draws away from his Creator, to Whom he has been commanded to cling and Whose ways he has been told to embrace. If we are remiss in this clinging to Hashem, we are, in effect, doing the opposite; we are drawing away from the Holy One.

When Moshe came to an inn on his way to redeem Israel and take them out of Egypt, *Hashem came upon him and wished to slay him* (*Shemos* 4:24). Moshe was travel worn and seems to have busied himself with the problem of lodging, in that first moment at the inn. All the merit he had accumulated in working on behalf of Israel was not enough to weigh the scales in his favor. At that moment his mind was removed from his mission and for this he was deemed blameworthy. That lack of total involvement in his mission constituted a drawing away from Hashem. At that very moment, Moshe was no longer fit to lead Israel out of Egypt, and it was then it was that *Hashem. . . wished to slay him*. With the circumcision of his son, Moshe returned to his former state and there was no further falling away from Hashem for the rest of his life.

See how great is the reward of a *mitzvah*. Who can comprehend it? The suspicion of the slightest trace of desire for money caused Yaakov to fear that his sons, the tribes of Hashem, would fall into the hands of Esav. All the merit of Yaakov, the most perfect of the forefathers, would not weigh in their favor. For that trace of desire for money, if it existed, would drive a wedge between Yaakov and the Creator.

If a slight fault such as this can have such an effect, how can we comprehend the result of even a slight movement towards the Holy One? For good is five hundred times more powerful than evil (*Sanhedrin* 101b).

With this thought, I have given you a great present, one, I believe, for which it is worthwhile that a man give half his possessions! And the whole idea is contained in a brief comment of *Chazal*.

> The Holy One made promises to two men and they were both fearful. The first was Yaakov, the chosen of the forefathers, of whom it is written, *Because Hashem chose Yaakov for Himself* (*Tehillim* 135:4). And the second was Moshe, the chosen of the prophets, as it is written, *Were it not for Moshe, His chosen* (ibid. 106:23). He does not say, "Fear not," except to the one who is fearful.
>
> (*Bereishis Rabbah* 76:1)

One could argue that because of their righteousness, they were fearful without cause. But the *Midrash* concludes, "How many times more so does this apply to us!"

(*Chochmah U'Mussar* I:75)

✌ Closing the Chest

R' YERUCHAM HALEVI OF MIR

And he rose that night and took his two wives and his two maidservants and his eleven children (Bereishis 32:23). And where was Dinah? He put her in a chest and locked it so that Esav would not see her. Yaakov was punished because he denied Dinah to his brother. Perhaps she would have brought him back onto the proper path. And she fell into the hands of Shechem (*Rashi* on *Bereishis* 32:23).

The Holy One said to him, "You prevented the possibility of a kindness to your brother; she will be taken by an enemy... You did not want her to marry one who is circumcised; she will marry one who is uncircumcised. You did not want her to be married in a permitted fashion; she will be married in a forbidden manner."

(*Bereishis Rabbah* 80:4)

Our master and teacher, R' Simchah Zissel of Kelm, commented: Wherein lies Yaakov's sin? He did as the *halachah* required him to do. For *Chazal* say that if one gives his daughter in marriage to a man who is ignorant, it is as if he ties her up and places her before a lion (*Pesachim* 49b).

Certainly Yaakov was obligated to lock Dinah in the chest. But he is faulted for a slight movement; he closed the chest a little more forcefully than was necessary, a movement so slight that only the Holy One could detect it. That is why he was punished. And how was he punished? With the Shechem chapter! That is the standard that the Holy One applies to the righteous.

(*Da'as Chochmah U'Mussar* I:84).

◂§ A Generation for Each Word

R' YOSEF LEIB BLOCH OF TELZ

Whered Yaakov called Esav "Master," the Holy One said to him,
"You humbled yourself before your brother and called him
'Master' eight times. I will cause eight kings to rise up from him,
before your sons, as it is written: *And these are the kings who ruled
in the land of Edom before a king ruled the children of Israel*
(*Yalkut Shimoni* on *Bereishis* 36:31). Because of the single expression
which escaped from Yaakov's lips, Israel's monarchy was post-
poned eight generations. Only at that later date was Yitzchak's
blessing, *Be lord over your brothers*, fulfilled (*Bereishis* 27:29).
When Yaakov humbled himself in word before Esav, it had an
effect on his soul, an effect which remained with his children for
eight generations.

In truth, Yaakov did not sin in calling Esav "Master." To the
contrary, *Chazal* see this chapter of the meeting of Yaakov and Esav
as a model of how we are to behave towards non-Jews in *golus* (see
Ramban). The *Yalkut* tells us that Rebbe wrote a letter to the
emperor, opening: "From your servant Yehudah to our master, the
emperor, Antoninus." He learned this from Yaakov's calling himself
"your servant" in Esav's presence.

Yaakov is held to account. For, had he been on an even loftier
plane than he was, Providence would have seen fit to deal with him
in a more elevated fashion. He would have been saved from Esav
without the need to humble himself.

Be that as it may, we see the effect of a single word of
self-abasement — the loss of kingship for eight generations.

(Shiurei Da'as I, *Omek Hadin)*

◄§ Eternal Punishment

R' SIMCHAH ZISSEL (THE ALTER OF KELM)

We do not bury a righteous man next to a wicked one, or even a righteous man next to one more righteous than he (*Yoreh Deah* 362:5). A man, probably, derives satisfaction from lying next to one who is like himself. Who knows how far this matter reaches?

There are four righteous pairs buried in the *Ma'aras HaMachpeilah*: Adam and Chavah, Avraham and Sarah, Yitzchak and Rivkah, Yaakov and Leah. Rachel, though she was Yaakov's principal wife, did not earn the right to lie next to her husband. And this, because, once, she had preferred to receive mandrakes to sleeping by her husband (*Bereishis Rabbah* 72:3), even though she did so for a lofty cause, for the sake of Heaven. Rachel was childless and the ancients had written that mandrakes help one conceive. In using them she was perfectly justified, for we are told not to rely on miracles but to make all possible efforts ourselves (*Taanis* 20b).

For this single act, an act which was not an intentional slight and which had a Heavenly purpose, she was punished eternally and denied the everlasting pleasure of lying close to her husband, the forefathers, and Adam, who had been formed by the Holy One Himself!

Rachel, but once, treated a righteous man lightly and was denied the privilege of lying near him forever. What, then, is the fate of one who treats the presence of Hashem in a light and degrading manner? Rachel was punished for a single misjudgment — involving not a matter of *halachah* — because she did not go beyond the letter of the law, as is the custom of the pious. What, then, is the punishment of one who errs in a matter involving a *halachah*, let alone an important *halachah* — and not one time only?

(Chochmah U'Mussar I:205)

✺ By a Hairsbreadth

R' SIMCHAH ZISSEL (THE ALTER OF KELM)

*L*eah went out to meet Yaakov (Bereishis 30:16). As a result, she gave birth to Yissachar whose offspring are described as *knowing to understand the times (Divrei HaYamim I* 12:32); Yissachar, who bends his shoulder to take up the yoke of Torah (*Rashi* on *Bereishis* 49:14).

The incident of Dinah begins: *And Dinah the daughter of Leah...* *went out... (Bereishis* 34:1). *Rashi* explains that she is called the "daughter of Leah" because she *went out* to see the daughters of the land; like mother like daughter.

What sin did Leah commit when she *went out* to meet Yaakov for the sake of a *mitzvah?* Why did this bring about the incident with Dinah which caused so much pain to Yaakov and the tribes, the incident which brought forth Yaakov's criticism — *Cursed be their anger for it is fierce (Bereishis* 49:7) — of Shimon and Levi. All that, because of the fine measure, the width of a hairsbreadth, which the Holy One applies to the righteous. Woe to us before the Day of Judgment, the Day of Reproof!

(Chochmah U'Mussar I:256)

◦§ Let Reuven Live and not Die

R' NOSSON TZVI FINKEL (THE ALTER OF SLOBODKA)

> *Chazal say: Whoever says that Reuven sinned is mistaken for it is said: And the children of Yaakov were twelve (Bereishis 35:23). This teaches us that they are all to be weighed at once [i.e. they were all still part of the same unit]. If so, what am I to make of: And he [Reuven] slept with Bilhah, his father's concubine (Bereishis 35:22). This tells us that he (Reuven) [somehow] disturbed the sleeping arrangements of his father (Shabbos 55b).*

[N]ote: When Rachel died, Yaakov moved his bed — which had always been in Rachel's tent — into Bilhah's. Reuven, feeling that his mother, Leah, had been shamed by being made subservient to Bilhah, a concubine, in this way brought this to his father's attention (see *Rashi* to *Bereishis* 35:22).]

Reuven, then, did not sin. On the contrary, he was involved in fulfilling the commandment of honoring his mother. And yet, the Torah views him as having fallen into a category of sin so serious that one should give up his life rather than transgress.

Reuven himself continued to do *teshuvah* from this sin, *And Reuven returned to the pit*. Reuven was not present when Yosef was sold. He was fasting while wrapped in his sackcloth for having disturbed his father's bed (see *Bereishis* 37:29 and *Rashi* ad loc.). And yet, despite his repentance, he thought that he was not one with his brothers, that he could not be numbered among them. For *Chazal* say: *And Reuven heard and saved him [Yosef] from their hand* (*Bereishis* 37:21). He [Reuven] said, "He [Yosef] counts me among his brothers, for it is written, ... *and eleven stars* (*Bereishis* 37:9); should I not then save him?" Though all the other brothers resented Yosef's having dreamt that they would bow down to him, Reuven, the firstborn, was thankful to Yosef for the dream. He thought that it was worth it to be told that all would bow down to Yosef, the child of Yaakov's old age, if, at the same time, he was informed that he was reckoned as one of the tribes (*Yalkut Shimoni* I:142)!

Reuven's "sin" was not a true sin. "Whoever says that Reuven sinned is mistaken." He fasted and wore sackcloth. Nevertheless his punishment is eternal. He lost forever the right of the firstborn and was denied the priesthood and the powers of a king (*Rashi* on *Bereishis* 49:3).

Nor was his "sin" forgiven. Generations later Moshe prayed for him: *Let Reuven live and not die* (*Devarim* 33:6) — i.e., let him live in this world and not die in the next. He prayed that the Bilhah incident not be remembered. *And may his men be numbered* (ibid.) — may he be numbered with his brothers and not be dropped from among them (*Rashi* ad loc.). In the words of the *Midrash:* "Had it not been for the tribes, Hashem would not have become reconciled to Reuven" (*Sifri* on *Devarim* 33:6).

How serious is even a mistaken act, even when done with good intention and for a *mitzvah*, and even though the Torah itself bears witness that there was no sin!

(Or HaTzafun I, Lashon HaTorah)

~§ Yaakov Wished to Live in Tranquility

R' YEHUDAH LEIB CHASMAN

Yaakov wished to live in tranquility. Why not? Did he not deserve tranquility in his old age after suffering at the hands of Esav and Lavan, after the defilement of Dinah and the loss of Yosef?

Man's purpose is not to attain that which he lacks; it is to serve Hashem in whatever situation he finds himself. *Chazal* say: *"With all your strength* (מְאֹדֶךָ)*";* with each measure (מִדָּה) that He measures out (מוֹדֵד) for you, praise (מוֹדֶה)Him exceedingly (*Berachos* 54a).

Yaakov wished to live in tranquility. He sought to become the likeness of the ideal man as depicted on the Heavenly chariot — which is his own likeness (*Chullin* 91b). It was the tranquility of the ideal which he sought, so that he might climb the ladder of the spirit — higher and higher. But Heaven was astonished by this request and a proclamation went forth from before Him: "Is that which is prepared for the righteous in the World-to-Come not sufficient for them? When Yaakov slept on the "rocks of the place" [and dreamt of the ladder] did not Hashem stand over him? Does he need a soft bed with a down quilt and feather pillows?"

And what was Heaven's answer to Yaakov's desire to live in tranquility? Immediately the anger of the brothers against Yosef was aroused and all peace was lost. He mourned for his son for many days; he refused to be comforted; the Divine spirit departed from him for twenty-two years; he thought that he might not be judged worthy to enter the World-to-Come. That was the answer.

It is as if he was told, "You wanted tranquility. There's your tranquility!" Awesome in the extreme! The Holy One is exacting to the width of a hairsbreadth when measuring the actions of the righteous. What a hairsbreadth and how exacting!

(*Or Yahel* III, *Vayeshev*)

↜§ Paid in Kind

R' CHAIM EPHRAIM ZAITCHIK

The Holy One pays in like kind — midah k'neged midah.
Because Yaakov tricked his father Yitzchak and caused
him to say, Are you my son Esav (Bereishis 27:21), the
Holy One repaid him in kind and caused him to say, It is
my son's tunic.

(*Bereishis 37:33; Torah Sh'lemah ch. 37*).

The Holy One said to Yehudah, "You do not have children and you do not know the heartaches children can bring. You caused [Yaakov] great pain when you tricked him, saying, *an evil animal has eaten him* (see *Bereishis* 37:20). Now you shall know the pain caused by children." And immediately thereafter we find: *And it was at that time [that] Yehudah descended. . .* (*Bereishis* 38:1).

Why are these considered actions which are "paid in kind?" What similarity is there between Yaakov's going to receive the blessings and his subsequent lament upon seeing Yosef's bloodied tunic? He approached Yitzchak only after his mother commanded him to do so, and only on the basis of her prophecy. And that approach was with trembling, weeping, and fainting. Two angels were needed to support him and help him on his way. Is there any comparison to the bitter keening of "my son's tunic" for the son of his old age? Did Yaakov's deception in these circumstances merit twenty-two years of mourning? And how can the misleading statement of *an evil animal has eaten him* — when Yosef was still alive — be compared to Yehudah's loss of two sons after his marriage?

And yet we are told that this is 'payment in kind.' How fearsome is the depth of judgment!

(*Mayanei Chaim, Vayeshev*)

❧ Yosef Has Been Sold for a Slave

R' NOSSON TZVI FINKEL (THE ALTER OF SLOBODKA)

Yosef the Righteous brought malicious gossip about his brothers to their father. Certainly there was no trace of malicious gossip in the *halachic* sense in his action. Since he was friendly with the sons of Bilhah, he did not reproach them before speaking to Yaakov, because he was certain that they would not listen to him. Yosef *brought* — rather than *took* — the malicious gossip; he brought it from one place to another, without adding to it. To *their* father — not to *his* father. It was for their benefit, in order that their father might reprimand them. Under such circumstances the prohibition against malicious gossip does not apply.

But Heaven saw in this a fault, albeit the slightest of the slight:

> You [Joseph] said that they treated the sons of the handmaidens in a derogatory fashion and called them slaves, [therefore] *Yosef was sold for a slave* (*Tehillim* 105:17). You said that they looked at the daughters of the land. By your life, I will sic the bear on you: *And his master's wife lifted her eyes to Yosef*.
>
> (*Bereishis Rabbah* 84:7)

Thus all Yosef's afflictions — his sale by his brothers, the attempted seduction by Potiphar's wife, the imprisonment — all stemmed from a fault so slight that no mortal could detect it, not even Yaakov. For Yaakov was not taken to task for listening to Yosef's gossip, nor did he reproach him.

Moreover, these painful sufferings were not sufficient to remove the stain. That stain remained for generations. In the chapter on the spies, Yosef's name is mentioned in connection with Menashe and not, as usual, with Ephraim: *For the tribe of Ephraim, Hoshea bin Nun... For the tribe of Yosef, the tribe of Menashe, Gadi ben Susi* (*Bamidbar* 13:8,11). The *Baalei Tosafos* comment: "Here

Yosef paid his debt for passing on malicious gossip. That is why his name is mentioned in association with the spy from the tribe of Menashe, whose leader was among those who spoke ill of the Land, and not with the tribe of Ephraim whose representative, Yehoshua, did not (see *Da'as Zekeinim Miba'alei HaTosafos* on *Bamidbar* 13:11).

The Red Sea was divided before the Children of Israel on the merit of Yosef (*Bereishis Rabbah* 87). Yet, because he passed on malicious gossip, out of the purity of his heart and for the purpose of having the matter corrected, he was sold as a slave and condemned to prison for eleven years. And finally, after all that, his "sin" was likened to the sin of the spies!

(*Or HaTzafun I, Z'chus V'Chovah*)

⧉ Yosef and His Brothers — The Slightest of Sins

R' SHLOMO HARKAVY

Shmuel bar Nachman said in the name of R' Yonasan: "When Yehudah and Yosef were arguing with one another, the angels said to each other, 'Come, let us descend and see the ox and the lion butting heads. Normally, the lion strikes terror into the heart of the ox and here they are contending with one another.'"

(*Tanchuma, Vayigash 4*)

The *Midrash* shows what an exalted plane the twelve tribes stood on. This was no debate or quarrel between two powerful men. The angels would not have descended to witness such a debate to see what would happen. We can only conclude that there is something which even the angels can learn and contemplate in a debate between the tribes. Every slight movement of the "tribes of Hashem" contains a Torah in its entirety.

It is written: *And Yosef brought malicious gossip about them to their father* (*Bereishis* 37:2). His brothers, we are told, subsequently judged him to be in the category of one who pursues another with the intention of killing him. The Sforno writes that after they had thrown Yosef into the pit, his brothers *sat down to eat bread* (*Bereishis* 37:25). They did not see what they had done as a tragedy, which might prevent them from eating bread together.

The righteous deny themselves food when a tragedy occurs because of them. That is how Israel acted when they nearly wiped out the tribe of Binyamin (see *Shoftim* 21:2) and Darius when he had Daniel thrown into the lions' den (*Daniel* 6:19). But Yosef's brothers had no such qualms. They viewed Yosef as a "pursuer." And the *halachah* concerning the "pursuer" is that he may be slain, if the pursued cannot be saved by another means (see Sforno on *Bereishis* 37:25).

It was as if they had passed sentence upon him in court. They saw themselves as performing a *mitzvah*: *And you shall eradicate the evil from your midst* (*Devarim* 13:6). Even after twenty-two years had passed and they had witnessed the great anguish that they caused their father Yaakov, they still did not question their deed.

When Yosef said that he would imprison one of the brothers, they said one to another, *Truly we are guilty with regard to our brother. We saw the pain of his soul when he entreated us and we would not listen* (*Bereishis* 42:21). The Sforno explains: "We were cruel to our brother. Though we judged him to be a 'pursuer,' we should have shown pity when he pleaded with us. It is for the cruelty which we revealed then, that this man acts cruelly towards us.

Even then they were still of the opinion that he deserved death. They regretted only their lack of pity. Only Reuven, who had not been partner to the sale of Yosef, argued differently: *Did I not say to you, "Do not sin against the lad," and now, indeed, his blood is demanded* (*Bereishis* 42:22). Again, following the Sforno, "It is not only the cruelty which is the sin, as you think, but 'his blood' — the sale itself was a spilling of innocent blood. He did not deserve the death penalty as you thought."

The judgment was so clear to them that when Yosef revealed himself to his brothers, they still wished to kill him, and an angel descended and scattered them to the four corners of the house (*Tanchuma Vayigash* 5).

The Alter of Kelm derives an important insight into human nature from this episode. When a man comes to a "first conception" on a matter, it takes root and becomes embedded in his consciousness. It then becomes a part of him. When confronted later with the same issue, he automatically acts in accord with his earlier decision, even if the original matter has long been forgotten. The judgment that Yosef deserved death was so rooted in the brothers' nature that even though they had gone to search for him and had decided to ransom him, no matter what the cost, immediately upon recognizing him, nature did its part and they wished to kill him. That "first conception" still held sway in their hearts. But they applied their intelligence to judge the issue once more.

How careful a man must be when he passes judgment on a matter on which he previously reached a strong "first conception." Unless he thinks very carefully, he cannot be critical, for he comes to the issue with his earlier prejudices.

The brothers had, in fact, been mistaken in their judgment. But their mistake had been so slight that it was very difficult for them to see it.

In the liturgical poem אֵלֶּה אֶזְכְּרָה, "These shall I recall," about the ten martyrs killed by the Romans, which we recite in the *Mussaf* of Yom Kippur (in some places, it is recited on every public fast day), we are told that when the High Priest, R' Yishmael was flayed, the angels cried out, "This is Torah and this is its reward?" Yet, the poem tells us at its beginning that the ten were martyred in retribution for the selling of Yosef. What room, then, was there for the angels' complaint? The Alter of Slobodka explained that the angels could not perceive any sin on the part of the brothers because whatever the sin was, it was so slight. In their opinion, the brothers were right.

In a similar vein, *Chazal* tell us (*Menachos* 29b) that when Moshe ascended to Heaven, he was shown R' Akiva in his greatness. He asked to be shown R' Akiva's reward and saw the Romans weighing R' Akiva's flesh in the butcher shops. Moshe then asked, "This is Torah and this is its reward?" Moshe could not comprehend the relationship between the selling of Yosef and the punishment meted out to the ten martyrs. The Holy One answered, "Silence, my son, silence! That is how it appears before me 'in the mind.'"

The Holy One did not arbitrarily silence Moshe. Hashem explained to him that the matter had left an impression in the World of Thought. When it filtered down through the lower worlds to that of action, the fault could no longer be detected for it was so slight. The suffering below was necessary to remove the impression above in the World of Thought.

We must also understand Yosef's "sin" when he told Yaakov that his brothers had fallen under suspicion of eating a limb of a living animal — not that they had eaten, but that they were suspect.

Rashi, indeed, says that they *had eaten* (*Bereishis* 37:2). To which the *Maharal* in *Gur Aryeh* comments: "*Rashi* went beyond the mark. Heaven forbid, that they ate; they were only suspect." And yet there is a *Midrash* that they did eat (*Tanchuma, Vayeshev* 3).

The *Mizrachi* argues that Yosef and his brothers differed on a point of *halachah*. They thought that what they were doing was permitted; he was of the opinion that it was forbidden. Yosef reprimanded them, as he was obligated to by the laws of reproof. When they were unwilling to accept his reprimand, since they thought they were right, he felt that he had no choice but to tell his father and save them from what he saw as a sin. It is likely that this was the result of his great love for them; he wished to save their souls from destruction. "Because Yosef was a perfect *tzaddik*, he was very strict in his observance of the laws of not eating from the living" (*Gur Aryeh* on *Bereishis* 37:2). And because he had such a high opinion of his brothers, he wished to prevent them from any taint of sin.

This can teach us an important lesson. Yosef the Righteous was punished with being sold into slavery, though he only wished to prevent his brothers from even a taint of sin, according to their elevated stature. He had exhausted every means at his disposal to prevent them from sinning. How much more so, then, should simple men question, examine and clarify the issue before they tell someone of the sin of another (*Me'Imrei Shlomo* 26).

R' YOSEF HOROWITZ (THE ALTER OF NOVARDHOK)

Because Yosef the Righteous said to the royal cupbearer:
Remember me... and mention me to Pharaoh (Bereishis 40:14),
two more years were added to his imprisonment.

Yosef certainly had not rebelled against Hashem as a consequence
of being imprisoned. He wished to be released from prison to rise to
even loftier heights in the world of the spirit. His attempts to gain
freedom, viewed in this light, seem more like a *mitzvah* than a sin.
And why do *Chazal* make the point that he was wrong to repeat the
request to be remembered, twice? [Note: Two words in the verse
have the root זָכֹר — remember: זְכַרְתַּנִי; וְהִזְכַּרְתַּנִי.] If asking to be
remembered (זְכַרְתַּנִי) was not a sin, what was wrong with seeking to
be mentioned (וְהִזְכַּרְתַּנִי)?

There are two obstacles to man's spiritual growth. (Wisdom itself
may stand in the way of spiritual growth.) There is a difference
between the wise man and a *talmid chacham*. Of the *talmid
chacham* it is said: "If you see a *talmid chacham* sin at night, do not
be suspicious of him on the following morning, for he has certainly
repented" (*Berachos* 19a). But of the wise man it is said: "When a
man has committed a sin and repeated it, it becomes a permitted act
in his eyes" (*Yoma* 86b). The sin becomes part of a systematic
approach. The sinner will justify his actions with all manner of
reasons as to why they are permitted.

When Yosef had only said, "remember me," he still had the
possibility of repenting for his concern with "tomorrow." But when
he said, "mention me to Pharaoh," he expanded upon his statement,
I was stolen from the land of the Hebrews (Bereishis 40:15). He has
already come to terms with the idea of relying on his own efforts to

obtain freedom. And thus, only after the second use of "remembering" was he faulted and punished.

But why was it invalid for him to take steps to help himself? We all do. There are many levels of trust in Hashem. Yosef stood on a very lofty plane in this respect. When his father sent him to see how his brothers were, the angel said to him: *I heard them say, "Let us go to Dosan"* (Bereishis 37:17). *Rashi* comments that the angel indicated to [Yosef] that [the brothers] were scheming against him and wished to kill him. But Yosef was steeped in faith and trust, and went to them. When the wife of Potiphar attempted to seduce him, he did not rely on his sense of spiritual immunity. He ran out without taking stock of the future. Great demands are made on one of such high stature.

Because Yosef made two requests of the royal cupbearer to try to free him, he was destined to remain in prison not for two weeks or two months, but for two more years! Such is the punishment for striving to help oneself in an improper manner. Not only does it not bring the goal nearer, it drives it off. "Honor flees from one who pursues it." He asked to be set free and instead was left in prison — one year for each attempt to be free.

(*Madregas Ha'adam, Darchei Habitachon* chapter 4)

ৰঙ্গ The Cost of a Single Movement

R' BEN ZION BRUK

And Yosef harnessed his chariot (Bereishis 46:29). Did he not have many servants? Love causes one to break the normal protocol.

(Bereishis Rabbah 55:8)

Did he not have a slave or servant to harness his chariot? This is to let us know that Yosef was greatly overjoyed and did not assume an air of majesty at that moment.

(Midrash HaGadol)

Yosef harnessed the chariot with joy. Did he not have several servants? This is the way he honored his father.

(Mechilta Beshalach on Shemos 14:6)

This deed was regarded so highly by the Holy One that *Chazal* tell us that the Yosef's act of harnessing his chariot to ride and meet his father negated Pharaoh's harnessing his chariot to pursue Israel (*Yalkut Shimoni, Vayera*).

And he went up towards Yisrael, his father, to Goshen and he appeared before him (Bereishis 46:29). Rashi comments, "He appeared before his father." What can *Rashi* be telling us by his comment? For if he went up towards his father, certainly he appeared before him.

The *mussar* thinkers have explained *Rashi*. He wished to emphasize that Yosef performed each act in order to give pleasure to his father. He wished his father to see *him*; his primary concern was not that he see *his father*.

Chazal tell us that two men experienced honor such as no others did. Of Yaakov it is written that when he came to Yosef, *Yosef harnessed his chariot and went up*. Who would see Yosef go forth and not go forth, too? Who would see the servants of Pharaoh, the palace elders and the elders of the land go forth and not go forth? This was done in order to fulfill that which is said: *The wise shall inherit honor* (*Mishlei* 3:35).

We see, then, how much Yosef strove to show honor to his father Yaakov, without giving thought to his own honor or pleasure. Is there anything missing?

And yet *Chazal* tell us: Why were Yosef's years shortened? Because he did not descend from the chariot in greeting his father. For it is said, *And [Yosef] fell upon [Yaakov's] neck* (*Bereishis* 46:29); he did so while as yet in the chariot (*Yalkut Temani* — cited by *Torah Shelemah* 46:176).

This shakes one to the depths of one's soul. Yosef the Righteous, as the Torah and *Chazal* tell us, did all that was possible to honor his father. And yet, because he neglected to perform one seemingly insignificant act, his life was cut short! Only the Torah could reveal such an insight. *Chazal* sensed the absence of a single word and learned a great lesson. For if the Torah took the trouble to inform us that Yosef himself harnessed his chariot, why did it not similarly tell us that he descended from the chariot to weep on his father's neck? That must have been omitted intentionally because in fact, he did not leave the chariot.

He did everything else that could be done, but this he did not do. He remained in his chariot and bent over to fall on Yaakov's neck. Most likely, he had thought it out carefully beforehand. For he was closely observed by his peers and each move would be carefully considered by the royal house.

In this one detail, he was niggardly in honoring his father, and for the lack of this single act, his life was cut short. How far Heavenly justice reaches!

(*Hegionei Mussar, Vayigash*)

⨳ A Year for Each Word

R' BEN ZION BRUK

When Yaakov said, *The days of my life are few and unhappy* (*Bereishis* 47:9), the Holy One said to him, "I saved you from Esav and Lavan and returned Dinah and Yosef to you, and yet you complain that your life has been short and full of evil? By your words, your days will be shortened by the number of years equal to the number of words between *And he said* (*Vayomer; Bereishis* 47:8) and *in the days in which they lived* (*Bereishis* 47:9)! You shall not live as long as your father Yitzchak!" There are thirty-three words in the verse. And it is by this number of years that Yaakov's life was shortened. For Yitzchak lived 180 years and Yaakov only lived 147 (*Midrash* cited by *Da'as Zekeinim Miba'alei HaTosafos*)

It is not for us to criticize Yaakov, but this can teach each of us a lesson. Imagine a man who suffered throughout his life. He felt hunger and distress; he was sent to extermination camps or Siberia; he was cut off from his beloved son for twenty-two years and had already mourned him as dead. Imagine all this and much more pain and tragedy besides. And then, he reaches *Eretz Yisrael*, a secure haven, and his son is returned to him. There are two sides to the coin of his life — the period of pain and suffering and that of joy and peace.

If the man were to complain of what he had gone through, he would be told, "Come now, look at the other side of the coin. You did have days of distress and poverty, but now your affairs are in order; you were at death's door in the extermination camps, but you were saved by Heavenly grace; you were terribly disturbed about your son, but now he has been returned to you. Be happy with your lot!"

And, indeed, the *Midrash* is a great object lesson for us. Yaakov's entire life was filled with pain and suffering. He was pursued by his brother Esav; he suffered at the hands of his uncle Lavan. As *Chazal* put it: *I was not at peace nor in tranquility and I did not rest and the disquiet came* (*Iyov* 3:26) — *I was not at peace* from Esav, *nor in tranquility* from Lavan *and I did not rest* from Dinah, *and the disquiet came* — the disquiet from Yosef came upon me (*Bereishis Rabbah* 84:3).

That was why Yaakov said, *The days of my life are few and unhappy*. His sorrows brought old age upon him and he appeared ancient (*Ramban* to *Bereishis* 47:9).

But because the Holy One applies a fine measuring rod to the righteous, Yaakov — the chosen one among our forefathers — was held to account for an expression that smacks of complaint. The Holy One told him, "Rather than cry out against the pains that have passed over you, rejoice that you have been saved from them."

There is a further point which bears examination. It is difficult to understand why Yaakov should have been held to account for the words spoken by Pharaoh: *And Pharaoh said to Yaakov: How many are the days of your life?* (*Bereishis* 47:8).

The early commentators explain that Pharaoh had never seen such an old man in Egypt. And Yaakov explained that old age had come upon him prematurely due to his many troubles (*Ramban* on *Bereishis* 47:9 and Sforno on *Bereishis* 47:8).

Yaakov was taken to task because he should have experienced joy and not become old in appearance. He should have looked youthful and vigorous. [That is why the verse of Pharaoh's statement makes up part of the thirty-three words which result in the shortening of Yaakov's life by thirty-three years. For Pharaoh saw him as an old man.]

This teaches us that no matter what the Holy One grants us, we should rejoice in our lot. Even if what we experience is very difficult, we should not show signs of the stress of seeking a livelihood, or of current anxieties.

(*Hegionei Mussar, Vayigash*)

ᵛᶟ Let Your Words Be Few

R' YEHUDAH LEIB CHASMAN

When Moshe Rabbeinu said [to the Holy One], *Why have You brought misfortune to this people (Shemos* 5:22), Hashem in His aspect of stern judgment wished to destroy Moshe. For it is said: *And Elokim [Hashem's name when he presents Himself as the enforcer of the Law] spoke to Moshe (Shemos* 6:3). But when the Holy One saw that he spoke thus because of Israel's suffering, He treated him in His aspect of compassion. For it is said: *And He said to him, I am Hashem (Shemos* 6:3; see *Shemos Rabbah* 6:7).

Moshe Rabbeinu was concerned heart and soul for Israel (see *Rashi* on *Shemos* 2:11). He was shattered by their pains and sought to understand their miserable condition. *Elokim* wished to apply the letter of the law. But Hashem, Who examines the innermost thoughts of a man, testified that Moshe spoke only because he felt Israel's suffering so acutely.

Nevertheless, the Torah tells us: *Your shall see what I shall do to Pharaoh (Shemos* 6:1). And *Chazal* interpret this to mean: You shall see the wars waged against Pharaoh but not those waged against the thirty-one kings [of Canaan]. Yehoshua, your disciple, will take vengeance upon them (*Shemos Rabbah* 5:23). For forty years Moshe was destined to carry the burden of Israel "as the nurse carries the nursing infant" and yet he was denied entry into the Holy Land. A multitude of prayers did not help and Hashem said to him, *Enough, speak no further to Me about this matter (Devarim* 3:26).

He had spoken up because he could not bear to see Israel in their suffering, and he was therefore prevented from seeing them in their joy. How frightening!

For Elokim is in the heavens and you are upon earth. Therefore, let your words be few (Koheles 5:1).

(*Or Yahel* III, *Shemos*)

ᴥ§ The Demand of Amalek

R' YEHUDAH LEIB CHASMAN

And Amalek came (Shemos 17:8). Where did they come from? They had gone to consult with Bilaam. And he advised them that they would be able to wage [a successful] war. For, he said, Israel's valor was due to their being descendants from Avraham. Since Amalek, too, belonged to Avraham's family they would be able to do battle with them.

(Esther Rabbah 7:13)

Amalek was a child of Timnah. Timnah was a princess, for it is written "Chief (*Aluf*) Timnah" (*Bereishis* 36:40). Chief (*Aluf*) denotes royalty, albeit, *uncrowned* royalty. Timnah approached Avraham, Yitzchak and Yaakov and asked that they convert her and bring her into the fold, but they were unwilling to accept her as a convert. Whereupon she became a concubine to Elifaz, the son of Esav, saying, "I would rather be a concubine to a member of Avraham's family than a princess in another nation." Because our forefathers rejected her, Amalek, who was to cause suffering to Israel, was born to her (*Sanhedrin* 99a).

Our forefathers were wholly committed to converting others. *And the souls which they created in Charan (Bereishis* 12:5) refers to the men converted by Avraham and the women converted by Sarah. Yet, here they are punished for rejecting a single woman! And most likely on good grounds! The later facts speak for themselves: she gave birth to Amalek. Still, the indictment stands. For it was in keeping with their great powers to turn the most corrupt, the future mother of Amalek, to the good. It was on this basis that Amalek came to do battle with Israel. They would make mention of the sin of the forefathers and thereby weaken Israel.

Moshe Rabbeinu said, *I shall stand on the top of the hill* (*Shemos* 17:9). *Top* (*rosh*), say *Chazal*, may be interpreted as the deeds of the Patriarchs, the hill (*givah*) may be understood as the deeds of the Matriarchs (*Mechilta* to *Shemos* 17:9). [In Bilaam's passages of blessing he says, "I see [Israel] from the top (*rosh*) of the cliffs and gaze upon him from the hills *[givaos]*." There, too, *rosh* and *givah* are understood as the Patriarchs and Matriarchs (see *Bamidbar* 23:9 and *Bamidbar Rabbah* 20:19).]

Moshe stood up and spoke of the worthy acts of the Patriarchs and Matriarchs. Amalek stood in opposition and charged, "And what about our mother, Timnah? They pushed her away from under the wings of the Divine Presence."

Therein lies the reason for the vast spilling of the blood of Israel by Amalek. How awesome is heavenly justice.

(*Or Yahel* I: 27-28)

✑§ It Will Be Very Stormy Round About Him

R' CHAIM SHMUELEVITZ

*And they saw the God of Israel. . . And He did not stretch
out his hand against the nobility of the children of Israel.
And they saw Elokim and they ate and drank (Shemos
24:10-11).*

*They deserved the death penalty, but the Holy One
did not wish to disturb the joy of [receiving] the Torah.
[He] waited until the dedication of the Mishkan to
[punish] Nadav and Avihu and until [that time when]
the people were like complainers (Bamidbar 11:1) to
punish the Elders. And the fire of Hashem burned among
them and consumed the edge (k'tzeh) of the camp,
(ibid.) — the leaders (ktzinim) of the camp.*

(Rashi on Shemos 24:10)

*And their sin? They looked upon Him with a coarse
heart, from the midst of eating and drinking.*

(Tanchuma cited by Rashi, on Shemos 24:11)

T he *Ibn Ezra* quoting R' Yehudah HaLevi explained that: The
Torah wrote, *And they saw Elokim and they ate and they
drank*, to tell us that although they had pleasure in being in the
Divine Presence they still needed to eat and drink, unlike Moshe
who did not eat or drink in the forty days during which he was on
Mount Sinai.

Nadav and Avihu and the Elders had reached the highest plane
that man can reach; they had *seen* Hashem, as it were. It is written,
For man cannot see Me and live (Shemos 33:20); and even of Moshe
it is said, *For he feared to look (Shemos 3:6)*. Yet they saw. But they
fell short of the level that Moshe attained when he went up on high

and experienced the Divine Presence. He reached such a level of sanctity that he lost all physical desire and had no need for food or drink at all. They, however, retained a measure of the material; they needed to eat and drink.

They had risen so high that they could gaze upon the Divine Presence, a state which requires purification of the physical and a refining of the soul. Yet, at that very same time, they still possessed an admixture of the material coarseness inherent in man; they had not shaken off all the dust of the physical. That is what is meant by the phrase "they looked upon Him with a coarse heart." That is why they were punished. And a terrible punishment it was — death by fire! All because they did not rise even higher. As *Chazal* have said, *It is very stormy round about Him* (*Tehillim* 50:3). This means that the Holy One applies a fine measuring rod, graduated in hairsbreadths, to the righteous (*Bava Kamma* 50a). [Note: By relating the similar sounding words in the phrases חוּט הַשַּׂעֲרָה (hairsbreadth) and וּסְבִיבָיו נִשְׂעֲרָה (stormy round about Him), they read the verse as if it said: those about Him — the righteous — are measured by the hairsbreadth.]

And even that slight measure of the physical which they still retained was related to the performance of a *mitzvah*, as the *Ramban* explains:

> *They ate and drank* means they ate flesh of sacrifices at the base of the mountain [*Sinai*] before Hashem, prior to returning to the[ir] tents...
>
> *And they drank* means that they rejoiced and had a festival (*Yom Tov*). For there is an obligation to rejoice upon receiving the Torah etc... R' Elazar says, "This is a source for the practice of holding a banquet on the completion of the Torah. "Thus we find when David contributed towards building the *Beis Hamikdash*: *And they sacrificed sacrifices to Hashem and offered up wholly burnt offerings to Hashem...They ate and drank before Hashem on that day with great rejoicing* (*Divrei HaYamim* I 29:21-22). And this is what they did here, too, on the day of the "marriage" of the Torah.

> (*Ramban* on *Shemos* 24:11)

The eating and drinking of the elders was, then, a *mitzvah*, like the banquet that one holds upon the completion of the Torah. They ate the meat of sacrifices, meat from the table of Heaven, so to speak. Where, then, was their sin?

This indicates that when we are told, *It is very stormy round about Him*, this may include an act which is a great *mitzvah* to men in general. The failure to perform that *mitzvah* would fly in the face of a clear *halachah*: we are told to hold a banquet upon the completion of the Torah and must do so. But for Nadav and Avihu and the Elders, who stood at the supreme height that a human being can attain, that same act of eating became a sin and they were held to account for it, as if it were the worst of capital offenses. They were expected to rejoice without eating and drinking since they had reached the state where they could see the Divine Presence. They serve as an object lesson for those who rise to lofty heights of Torah and fear of Heaven. Such men will be prosecuted severely for a minute falling away from what is fitting — each one in accordance with the level he has attained.

It is in this light that we can understand R' Eliezer's comment to R' Akiva, "Yours is far harder than theirs" (*Sanhedrin* 68a). And so it was. They tore at his flesh with iron combs (*Berachos* 61b) and his flesh was weighed out in the butcher shops (*Menachos* 29b). And the reason? Because "Your heart is as wide open as an assembly hall. If you would have served me [as a disciple], you would have learned much Torah" (*Rashi* on *Sanhedrin* 68a).

Yet R' Akiva had no choice. He could not serve R' Eliezer, had he wanted to. R' Eliezer had been placed in excommunication. Nevertheless, the demand that he rise even higher in Torah still stands. And it is of R' Akiva that we are speaking, of whom Moshe said when he stood before the Holy One, "You have a man like him and you are giving the Torah through me" (*Menachos* 29b)? It was because of his potential greatness, because his heart was as wide open as an assembly hall that such a demand could be made. He was fit to attain even more than he did.

It was ordained that Chaninah ben Tradiyon, who taught Torah in public in a time of religious persecution, when it was forbidden to do so, be condemned to death by fire because he uttered the

Ineffable Name with its proper pronunciation. Though this is generally forbidden, he had done it to learn how to pronounce the Name, and that is permitted. It is forbidden to learn the proper pronunciation in order to use it, but you may do so in order to understand and teach. *Rashi* comments that though he acted in a permitted fashion — he pronounced it properly to learn — the Holy One applies a measuring rod graduated in hairsbreadths to the righteous and even such a permitted act is suspect in their case (see *Avodah Zarah* 18a and *Rashi* ad loc.).

Here, again death by fire is ordained because of a minute fault.

(Sichos Mussar 5732, no. 20)

ᵫ§ The Punishment Fits the Crime

R' CHAIM EPHRAIM ZAITCHIK

A wise woman asked R' Elazar, "Since all who sinned in worshiping the Golden Calf committed the same sin, why were their punishments different?" [We find death by the sword: *Let each gird his sword on his hip...* (*Shemos* 32:27); death by plague: *And Hashem plagued the nation...* (*Shemos* 32:35); death by dropsy: *And he spread [the powder ground from the Golden Calf] upon the face of the waters...* (*Shemos* 32:20).]

R' Elazar answered, "Those who slaughtered the sacrifices and offered up incense were slain by the sword; those who hugged and kissed the Calf, by the plague; those who felt joy in their hearts, by dropsy" (see *Yoma* 66b and *Rashi* ad loc.). Each received his just punishment.

They descended into the depths like a stone... (*Shemos* 15:5). *They plummeted like lead...* (*Shemos* 15:10). *Your anger will consume them like straw* (*Shemos* 15:7). The wholly evil were treated like straw, tossed up and down until they were broken in body; those who were not wholly evil sank like stone; and the best of them sank immediately like lead (see *Sanhedrin* 46a). The Holy One weighs the punishment exactly to fit the sin.

And he [the murderer] shall remain there until the death of the High Priest. . . (*Bamidbar* 35:25). It has already been explained that the unintentional murderer is exiled. Since unintentional murders are not all identical — for some are closer to accidents while others approach intentional murder — the length of exile is not identical for all. For some murderers, their exile begins shortly before the death of the High Priest; others die while in exile, before the High Priest. This is the punishment meted out by Hashem, Who knows and bears witness; He punishes each one in accordance with his degree of negligence (Sforno on *Bamidbar* 35:25).

R' Ada of Yafo said: "The names of the ten sons of Haman and the word 'ten' (*Megillas Esther* 9:7-10) must be read in a single breath. Why? Because all departed life at the same instant" (*Megillah* 16b). They were alike in their evil and they received identical punishments.

R' Yose ben Chalafta said: "Whoever knows how many years Israel worshiped idols knows when the son of David [i.e., *Mashiach*] will come" (Introduction to *Eichah Rabbah*). The length of our Exile, its pains and sufferings, are measured exactly in accordance with the sin, down to the last hairsbreadth!

(*Kol Tzofa'ich* III, *Averos V' Onashim*)

◆§ A Taint of Negligence

R' SIMCHAH ZISSEL (THE ALTER OF KELM)

A nd the princes brought... R' Nasan said: What prompted the princes to be the first to contribute at the dedication of the Altar and yet not towards the building of the *mishkan?* They said, "Let the general public contribute whatever they wish and we will supply whatever is lacking." But since the public contributed all that was necessary (*Shemos* 36:7), the princes had nothing to do but bring the onyx stones. That is why they were the first to contribute to the dedication of the Altar. Because they were sluggish in the building of the *Mishkan*, a letter was left out of their title; it is written: הַנְּשָׂאָם — and not הַנְּשִׂיאָם (*Rashi on Shemos* 35:27).

The princes said, "Let them contribute and we will make up whatever is lacking." They would have given a treasure equal to that given by the nation as a whole, had that been necessary. But, because they waited and did not contribute immediately, the Torah found a taint of laziness. And for that, a letter of their title was dropped from the Torah for eternity!

(*Chochmah U' Mussar* II: 107).

◆§ Great Is the Deed and Great Is the Demand

R' BEN ZION BRUK

The building of the *Mishkan* was so dear to the Holy One that its details were repeated five times in the Torah. According to the *Ramban*, Hashem desired the work and mentioned it in His Torah so many times to increase the reward of those involved in its construction.

Special intention was required in all the phases of the work. The Torah says, *They take for Me* (*Shemos* 25:1), to which *Rashi* comments, *for Me* — "with Me in mind." On the verse, *They will make a Mikdash for Me* (*Shemos* 25:8), *Rashi* similarly comments, "They will make a house of holiness with Me in mind."

We find similar remarks with reference to the special clothing of the High Priest. The *Ramban* writes on the verse, *And you shall make garments for your brother Aharon for honor and glory* (*Shemos* 28:2). *For honor and glory* means that they should fashion holy garments for Aharon to serve in them for the *honor* of Hashem, Whose presence is in their midst, and for the *glory* of their strength, as it is written, *For You are the glory of their strength* (*Tehillim* 89:18). So, too, the clothes of a regular *kohen* are described as "for honor and glory." All the clothes had to be made specifically as clothing for the *kohen*. That is why it says, *And you shall speak to the wise of heart, whom I have filled with the spirit of wisdom, that they should understand what they are to do* (*Shemos* 28:3).

The Sforno also comments: *for honor* — for the honor of G-d, may He be blessed, since they are garments of holiness for His service. And similarly on the verse, *and they shall take the gold...* (*Shemos* 28:5), he adds, "When they take the gold, they should have the same thoughtful purpose that they do when they fashion it."

The work was done with a specific purpose in mind and pure intent was required throughout the labor, from start to finish. And if Israel did find favor and the Divine Presence did rest upon their creations — *And the glory of Hashem filled the Mishkan (Shemos 40:34)*, this is proof positive that all was done as perfectly as possible. For had there been some slight lack, a tiny fault, they would not have attained the level of "I shall rest among them." The Torah repeats 'as Hashem commanded Moshe' several times, and we read: *Everything, exactly as Hashem commanded Moshe, thus did the Children of Israel do all the work (Shemos 39:42)*. Elsewhere the Torah tells us: *And Moshe saw all the labor and they had done it as Hashem had commanded; thus they had done it (Shemos 39:43)*.

The Sforno remarks upon this singleness and purity of purpose: In every act the intent of the artisans was *to do G-d's will* as He had commanded Moshe. Though the artisans did the work, all of Israel participated in the building of the *Mishkan*. Some had contributed money and some did the work in the generosity of their hearts in order to fulfill the will of their Creator (Sforno on *Shemos* 39:5 and 39:32).

Chazal have said: "Do not say that Bezalel alone was favored with wisdom." The Holy One gave wisdom, understanding and knowledge to everyone who was involved in the work of the *Mishkan*, as it says, *And all the wise of heart did (Shemos 36:8)*. And do not think that wisdom was granted only to human beings; even the animals [were granted wisdom], as it says, *wisdom and understanding* בְּהֵמָה — *in them (Shemos 36:1)*. The latter is read as בְּהֵמָה — *animal (Yalkut Shimoni 411)*.

(The donkey of Pinchas ben Yair knew whether the *maaser* had been taken or not from the feed placed before him (*Chullin 7a*). And the oxen which drew the wagon carrying the Ark of the Covenant, back from captivity by the Philistines, understood immediately what precious cargo they were pulling. To honor the Ark, they turned their heads back to face the Ark, as it says, *And the oxen went straight,* וַיִּשַּׁרְנָה (*Shmuel I 6:12*). What is meant by וַיִּשַּׁרְנָה? The oxen opened their mouths and sang a song (שִׁירָה) of praise (see *Tanchuma, Vayakhel 7*). Animals, too, can be granted wisdom and understanding.)

Israel was quick to perform the *mitzvah* of building the *Mishkan*. In a single day they brought all the necessary contributions to the Tent of Meeting; Moshe commanded that the contributions be brought to the artisans until [the artisans] told Moshe that the people had brought enough (see *Ramban* on *Shemos* 36:3).

After all this, we are seized by trembling when we hear what *Chazal* have said: R' Yochanan ben Pazi said in Rebbe's name, "Can we read these verses and not feel shame? To perform a *mitzvah* it appears that only some participated: *And everyone who was generous of heart* (*Shemos* 35:22), i.e., only the generous of heart contributed to the building of the *Mishkan*, not everyone. But for a heinous sin, all participated: *And the whole nation took off* [the gold jewelry for the Golden Calf] (*Shemos* 32:3)."

The prophet Zephaniah also reproached them. They rose early to sin with the Golden Calf, but not to build the *Mishkan*. Of the Golden Calf it says, *They rose early the next day* (*Shemos* 32:6). But when they contributed to the building of the *Mishkan* we do not find any mention of an early hour: *And they brought another contribution to him each morning* (ibid. 36:3; see *Talmud Yerushalmi, Shekalim* 1:1 and *Korban HaEidah* ad loc.).

Even those who did respond to the call to contribute to the *Mishkan* were found lacking in some respect by *Chazal*. They were, indeed, diligent in the extreme. They gave generously and brought what they offered daily, morning after morning (בַּבֹּקֶר בַּבֹּקֶר). When the word בַּבֹּקֶר is repeated, it indicates an earlier hour than that signified by the single use of the word בקר (see *Pesachim* 59a). And yet, *Chazal* complain that they did not rise *early*, as did those who sinned with the Golden Calf. This it is that causes *Chazal* to tremble and to demand that we, too, tremble in shame!

R' Eliezer the Great said that no one ever came to the *beis midrash* in the morning before him. Nor had he ever dozed, even momentarily, in the *beis midrash*. He was always the last to leave and never engaged in a casual conversation while there.

But we find elsewhere another comment of R' Eliezer: "In all my days no one ever came to the *beis midrash* earlier than I. Once, I arose early and saw those who carry the cut foliage and straw out to the fields for fertilizer, and I said to myself, *If you seek it [the wisdom of Torah] like silver and search it out like hidden treasure, then you will understand the fear of Hashem* (*Mishlei* 2:4-5). We are not even like those who carry out the foliage and straw" (*Shir HaShirim Rabbah* 1:1-9). He castigated himself for having found the common laborers going about their mundane tasks, while he was not yet learning Torah. The verse demands that we *seek [Torah] like silver* at all times.

Such is the approach of those holy figures who do not say, "Enough," when it comes to service of Hashem. No matter how much they have done, they still desire more. Just as the average man is never sated with his material attainments, they are not satisfied with *mitzvos* and Torah, and always seek more and more.

(Hegionei Mussar, Vayakhel)

◆§ Why Have You Not Eaten

R' SIMCHAH ZISSEL (THE ALTER OF KELM)

L et us picture a man in pain, bent by hard and bitter suffering. Imagine that someone berates him for not eating *matzah*. Would this not appear to us as cruel? Why should he speak harshly to a man whose soul drinks bile? The Holy One Himself would not criticize his creations so sharply!

But what happened when two of Israel's shining lights, Nadav and Avihu, fell; when they died an unnatural death, on the day of Israel's rejoicing? Though his pain and suffering were great, Aharon did not question the ways of Hashem; he saw himself as the cause of their death. Nevertheless, Moses spoke angrily to him, *Why have you not eaten the sin offering* (*Vayikra* 10:17)? Aharon and his remaining sons could not excuse themselves by saying that they had forgotten to do so in their mental anguish. They were like soldiers in the service of their king. Private suffering is no answer for being absent without leave. Soldiers are meant to dedicate themselves body and soul to the king and to be unmindful of personal hurt. This should serve as an example of what is meant by accepting the authority of the Heavenly kingdom in its fullest sense.

(Chochmah U'Mussar I:238).

◆§ Like the Child Who Runs out of the Classroom

R' NOSSON TZVI FINKEL (THE ALTER OF SLOBODKA)

*A*nd *they traveled from the mountain of Hashem* (*Bamidbar* 10:33). They ceased to follow after Hashem and veered away (*Shabbos* 116a). The *Ba'alei Tosafos* explains that they left Sinai, like the child who races from the classroom at the end of the school day.

Had it not been for this sin, they would have immediately entered the Holy Land (*Ramban* on *Bamidbar* 10:35). Yet, when the Ark traveled, were they not required to travel, too? What then, was their sin? Certainly, the fact of leaving Sinai was not by itself held against them. On the contrary, they were on the way to their goal, to the Land of Israel. "Had they been found worthy they would have entered *Eretz Yisrael* in three days' time" (*Yalkut Shimoni* I:727).

But Heaven compared the force Moshe had used to remove them from collecting the booty of Egypt, which they found strewn on the shore of the Sea (*Rashi* on *Shemos* 15:22), to their lightheartedness in leaving Sinai. At the Sea, Moshe had to compel them to cease from their gathering booty; at Sinai there was no need to force them to leave against their desires. Even though they were on the way to the Chosen Land, even though they traveled by command of the Divine Presence, their lightheartedness made it seem as though they were turning away from Hashem.

(Or HaTzafun I, M'nias Chesed)

◄§ Eternal Weeping

R' ELIYAHU ELIEZER DESSLER

Israel said: "Moshe Rabbeinu, let us send men before us" (Devarim 1:22). "Why?" said Moshe.

Because the Holy One has promised us that we will enter the land of Canaan and inherit all that is good... They are hiding their money and we won't be able to find it. The promise of the Holy One will, then, not be fulfilled. Let spies go and "dig out" (וְיַחְפְּרוּ; see Devarim 1:22) information; they will see where the Canaanites are hiding their treasures. When Moshe heard that, he was taken in (Devarim 1:23): And it was good in my eyes.

(Yalkut Shimoni, Shlach 742).

The generation of the desert, the generation of wisdom and awareness of G-d, convinced themselves that they wished to send spies only so that the words of the Holy One would not fall by the wayside. And Moshe Rabbeinu, despite the depth of his wisdom, did not see their error. If Moshe could not discern their error — that slight inclination to involve themselves directly in the Divine design of things — how could Israel, then, be held accountable?

The *Maharal* writes in his *Gur Aryeh* that the spies were righteous, but because those who sent them were evil, the spies became evil too. The evil of Israel penetrated their messengers, the spies, and caused them to sin. This in turn brought about their own unnatural deaths, the death of the entire generation in the desert, and the weeping on that day throughout the ages.

When self-interest clouds one's judgment, it does not wholly obscure the truth. Even when man's desire persuades him that the false is true, he knows within himself that the truth has more of verity about it. Because of this, he is called to account. "Why," he is asked, "did you not look at yourself, through the lens of truth?"

(Michtav M'Eliyahu I:62,192)

⇥ Enough!

R' ELIYAHU LOPIAN

*A*nd *Hashem said to me, "Enough! Don't continue to speak to me about this" (Devarim 3:26).* R' Levi said: [Moshe] told them, "Enough," and he was told, "Enough." He told them, *Enough, sons of Levi (Bamidbar 16:7);* he was told, *Enough* [of your prayers]! (*Sotah* 13b).

Moshe said, "Enough," to the Levites who joined with Korach to seek the *kehunah* and the Holy One, Who is exact to the hairsbreadth in dealing out justice to the righteous, framed his punishment with a statement using that exact expression.

Just think! Moshe, the trusty shepherd of his people, prayed to Hashem, "Let Moshe and a thousand like him perish, but let not one fingernail of Israel be harmed." Moshe prayed on their behalf for forty days until fire seized his bones because of the sin of the Golden Calf (*Berachos* 32a). He prayed for them when they cried after hearing the report of the spies and when they complained of a lack of food. Now, with this fourth incident, when the stink of sin arose from Korach and his supporters, he was already wearied (*Rashi* on *Bamidbar* 16:4).

He approached them and tried to calm them with soft words (see *Yalkut Shimoni* I:750). Korach answered not a word. And Moshe still did not become angry, but pleaded with them: "Enough" — let the honor that you have attained be sufficient for you; don't ask for more. And for this "Enough," great charges were hurled at him. Though he begged at length to be allowed to enter the Holy Land, the Holy One replied: "Enough" — just as you told Korach and his camp that they should be satisfied with what they had, and not to seek more, don't ask to be allowed to set foot into the Land. It is enough for you to remain in the desert.

(*Lev Eliyahu* III:114)

⊷§ Through the Generations

R' SIMCHAH ZISSEL (THE ALTER OF KELM)

T he followers of Korach were very important individuals —
*princes of the assembly, who were called upon in times of need;
men of reputation (Bamidbar* 16:2). They mistakenly thought that
what they were doing was for the sake of Heaven. They wanted to
serve Hashem, to be *kohanim.* That each agreed to bring his censer
on the morrow is proof of this. Each thought Hashem would choose
him. And because of their pure motive the censers were sanctified.

And yet Rabbah bar bar Channah said: "Once we were in the
desert. . . and [an Arab merchant] said to me, 'Come, I'll show you
those who were swallowed up with Korach.' I saw two cracks and
smoke came forth from them. He said, 'Listen! What do you hear?'
And I heard them say that Moshe is true and his Torah is true. And
he told me that every thirty days the hellfires of *Gehinnom* bring
them back to this place and they say Moshe is true and his Torah is
true. . ." (*Bava Basra* 74a). From the time of Moshe until that of
Rabbah bar bar Channah they suffered, even though they sinned
unintentionally.

(*Chochmah U'Mussar* I:117)

◄§ You Are Always Angry

R' YOSEF LEIB BLOCH

Pinchas ben Elazar turned away My anger from upon the Children of Israel (Bamidbar 25:11).

The situation was grave, the anger devastating. Tens of thousands of Israel had worshiped the idol of Ba'al Peor, with the most degrading and revolting forms of idol worship of all. A prince of Israel stood up contemptuously against Moshe Rabbeinu and no one rose to challenge him. Only Pinchas "saw the deed and remembered the halachah." His mind was clear; he rose zealously, seized by the anger of Hashem, and experienced ten miracles. The plague was halted and Hashem said, Behold I give my covenant peace to him (Bamidbar 25:12).

Pinchas is Eliyahu. After Eliyahu brought about Hashem's destruction of the priests of Ba'al, he fled to the cave to escape Jezebel. There he was asked, What are you doing here Eliyahu? And he answered, "I was angry for Hashem, the G-d of Hosts, for the Children of Israel abandoned Your covenant, cast down Your altars and slew Your prophets by the sword" (Melachim I 19: 9-10).

He should have said: "Master of the Universe, behold Your children, the children of Avraham, Yitzchak, and Yaakov, who did Your bidding in Your world." But he did not do so. He had said, "I was angry."

And [the angel] said to him, "You are always angry! At Shitim you were angry because of licentiousness; here, too, you are angry" (Yalkut Shimoni II:217).

Pinchas/Eliyahu is being held to account for his anger in the desert, though it was precisely that zealous anger which turned back the anger of Hashem, and caused him to be granted eternal priesthood. Some fault was found. He should have had more of an element of tenderness, of delicacy. "You are always angry." How deeply justice searches!

⋖§ The Angels Wished to Push Him off

R' AVRAHAM GRODZINSKI

The angels wished to push Pinchas off. And the Holy One said to them, "Leave him be. He is a zealot, son of a zealot. He turns back anger and is the son of one who turns back anger."

The tribes began to speak contemptuously and shame him, "Look at this one whose mother's father [Yisro] fattened calves for slaughter to idols. He has killed a prince of Israel." And so the Torah gives Pinchas' family tree: *Pinchas, the son of Elazar, the son of Aharon the priest* (*Bamidbar* 25:11).

Six miracles were performed for Pinchas and the plague was halted on his behalf (see *Sanhedrin* 82b). He was granted eternal priesthood (*Zevachim* 101).

Why then did the angels wish to push him off? Did they not want Zimri to be punished; did they wish the plague to continue to rage? The tribes shamed him by speaking of Yisro, Moshe's father-in-law, who had converted, though you are forbidden to say to a *baal teshuvah*, "Remember your former deeds," let alone to his grandchild. And the Holy One had to reply and set forth Pinchas' family tree. Killing is an improper act. Therefore, even when done with a proper motivation, zealousness on behalf of Heaven, it must be performed with complete purity of heart. Yael saved Israel through a sin which was committed for the sake of Heaven. *Chazal* ask, "But did she not have pleasure?" To which they answer, "For the righteous any benefit from the wicked is an evil" (*Nazir* 23b). Were this not so, Yael would have been forbidden to act as she did, for Israel cannot be saved through that which is forbidden and Heaven finds favor in the eyes of man only through the deeds of a worthy agent. Thus *Rabbeinu Yonah* writes (*Shaarei Teshuvah* 3:219): "One should reveal hypocrites who act as though they are righteous, since not doing so may bring about the desecration of Hashem's name when Hashem punishes them in a way which seems undeserved" (*Yoma* 83b). Yet he who is not free from the same sin should not be the one to reveal them.

Yehu was commanded to slay the house of Achav. But when he behaved in the same manner as Achav had, he was viewed as a murderer. The *Semak* derives a *halachah* from this: If a man kills a pursuer in order to save the man being chased, but is himself guilty of the same sin as the pursuer, he is viewed as having spilled innocent blood (*Mitzvah* 83).

If purity of heart is crucial, so, too, is family background. If there is some flaw in the past — even in a grandfather — that calls into question one's purity of heart. Know that the acts of the fathers affect their descendants! The proof is from Balak, King of Moav. *Chazal* said: A man should busy himself constantly with Torah and *mitzvos*, even if it is not for their own sake. Even if in the beginning, he does not learn and observe the *mitzvos* for their own sake, he will be led to perform them for their own sake. Because Balak, King of Moav, offered up forty-two sacrifices, he was found worthy to have Ruth as a descendant. And Shlomo, whom it is said sacrificed a thousand wholly burnt offerings, was, in turn, a descendant of Ruth.

Balak was far from offering sacrifices for their own sake. His intention was evil; he wished to curry favor with Hashem so that Hashem would agree to destroy Israel. This is like one who learns Torah in order to be able to criticize and vex others. That is forbidden and of such a person it is said it would be better had he not been created (*Tosafos*, *Berachos* 17a). And for a non-Jew it is forbidden to do an act which is not for its own sake. Koresh, for example, was viewed as an evil man because he sent sacrifices to the *Beis Hamikdash* so that the *kohanim* would pray that he live a long life.

Despite all this, Balak was rewarded. Generations later, Shlomo sacrificed his thousand offerings in holiness and purity for their own sake.

Pinchas did a great deed and fulfilled a *halachah* received by Moshe at Sinai. Zimri deserved to be killed, but not by the son of a woman whose father had worshiped idols before his conversion! That is why the Torah gives Pinchas' pedigree back to Aharon, who loved peace and pursued peace. This shows his purity of heart. Had this not been so, had there been the smallest taint, which had been passed on from his grandfather, Pinchas would have been committing murder!

(Toras Avraham, Toras Emes 5)

⋞ Moshe Began to Fear

R' SIMCHAH ZISSEL (THE ALTER OF KELM)

I have caused you to see with your eyes (Devarim 34:4). This teaches us that the Holy One showed Moshe Gehinnom.

"Who is judged there?" asked Moshe. "The wicked and those who sin against Me, as it is said, And they will go out and see the corpses of the men who sinned against Me (Yeshayahu 66:24)." When Moshe began to fear Gehinnom, Hashem said, I have caused you to see with your eyes and you shall not cross over to there (Devarim 34:4).   (Bamidbar Rabbah 23:5).

*E*ach of us should be seized with shuddering when we read this. The Holy One said: "The wicked and those who sinned against me." Of Moshe it is said: *In My entire house, he is true (Bamidbar 12:7).* Why should he of all people have feared? It would seem that the mere sight of *Gehinnom* caused his fright — he, too, feared its punishment, *for no man shall stand righteous before You.*

And it might be that Moshe was shown the sufferings of *Gehinnom* in terms of what *Chazal* call the "deepening of *Gehinnom*" (*Eruvin* 19a). There are infinite depths with regard to the pains of *Gehinnom*. And the depth is measured in small fractions, dependent on the intensity of the sin.

When he was shown *Gehinnom*, the infinite gradation of sin was impressed upon Moshe more than it had been previously. Thus, even when the Holy One assured him that the wicked and the sinners are judged there, Moshe still feared that Hashem might judge him with extreme exactness. As *Chazal* say, "No promises are made to the righteous" (*Bereishis Rabbah* 76:2).

This shows us that the greater the depth of the sin, the greater the depths of *Gehinnom* which await the sinner. Man should fear greatly because of a sin. Who knows what depths of the pain are being prepared?

The Waters of Strife (מֵי מְרִיבָה) can give us some idea of the infinitesimal gradations of a sin. We cannot really understand Moshe and Aharon's sin. We do not know why speaking to the stone sanctifies the name of Hashem more than does striking it. Moshe, indeed, assumed when he was told, *Take the staff* (*Bamidbar* 20:8), that he was to strike the rock with it. Can there be a sin more unintentional than his? And yet he was punished so severely that all his pleading to enter the Land was to no avail (*Devarim Rabbah* 11:10).

The worst punishment is to be described by the Torah as having sinned when a sin has not really been committed. *Chazal* tell us, "Whoever says that Shlomo sinned is mistaken." When we are told that his wives turned aside his heart (*Melachim* I 11:4), what is meant is that they *wished* to turn his heart aside, but, in truth, they did not (*Shabbos* 56b). Nevertheless, *Chazal* say that it would have been better had Shlomo been a cleaner of sewers rather than to have had this verse written about him (*Shemos Rabbah* 6:1).

Think of what Shlomo did in terms of improving the kingdom, of the degree of the sanctification of the name of Hashem for which he was responsible, of how greatly he raised the honor of Israel — and the honor of Israel is the honor of Hashem. Remember that he obtained the *shamir* (the worm which could cut through stone) with great effort and wisdom in order to build the *Beis Hamikdash* and he succeeded in building it. It was not without reason that the great men of his time — the prophet Nasan among them — put their lives on the line in order to have him crowned. And yet the *Midrash* says that he would have been more fortunate to be a cleaner of sewers and not have the verse written about him. And he did not even sin. The *Gemara* (*Shabbos* 56b) is even harsher than this *Midrash:* Better had he been a servant in the service of idols and not to have had it written about him that *he did wickedness in the eyes of Hashem* (*Melachim* I 11:6). There seems no end to the punishment for a sin.

Of Moshe and Aharon it is written, *Because you did not believe in Me* (*Bamidbar* 20:12); *Because you betrayed Me* (*Devarim* 32:51); *When you rebelled against Me* (*Bamidbar* 27:14). These are verses written about sacred figures, even though their sin was unintentional. Hashem had said, *Take the staff*; these were grounds for error. Yet, it was perhaps this sin that led Moshe to fear *Gehinnom*, so much so, that the Holy One had to assure him, "You shall not cross over to there."

We are not told that Hashem said: "Moshe! What are you afraid of! Is *Gehinnom* created for the likes of you? Of My entire household, aren't you the one who is true? How could you even begin to be afraid?" No! He gave a promise, "You shall not cross over there."

Let those who are as brave as lions fear; let the mighty feel shattered and their hearts melt within them!

(*Chochmah U'Mussar* I:36)

ᴥ§ Thorns in Your Eyes

R' NOSSON TZVI FINKEL (THE ALTER OF SLOBODKA)

The Holy One said to Rachav: You said, Because Hashem, your Elokim is the Elokim in the heavens above and the earth below (Yehoshua 2:11). As far as earth is concerned, fine! But when you speak of the heavens, you speak of that which you have not seen. By your hand, your son shall stand and see what prophets have not seen, as it says, The heavens opened and I saw visions of Elokim (Yechezkel 1:1).

(Yalkut Shimoni II:10)

Eight prophets and the prophetess Chuldah were among Rachav's descendants (*Megillah* 14b). Can we, then, judge who she really was?

For their part, the Children of Israel, who were kind to her and granted her life, were bound to do so. They had an obligation to show their gratitude. Thus, we find that when the tribes of the Children of Yosef went up to attack Beis El and met an inhabitant of the city, they saved him and his family in return for showing them the approach to the city. They then slew the rest of the populace. The one they spared made his way to the land of the Chitim and established Luz, where the dye, *techeles*, was produced. Luz was immune to conquest and the Angel of Death had no entry there (*Shoftim* 1:22-26; *Yalkut Shimoni* II 38).

The Children of Yosef did not act according to the command, *You shall not allow any soul to live* (*Devarim* 20:16), which applies to the Canaanites. On the contrary, they granted the man who helped them life without end, for doing no more than pointing a finger in the right direction. How much more so did Rachav, who endangered her life and saved the spies, deserve Israel's gratitude and kindness in return. And yet *Chazal* say:

> The Holy One said: I told them, "*If you will not drive out the inhabitants of the land. . . they will be thorns in your eyes and stings in your sides*" (*Bamidbar* 33:55). Yet they did not do so; Yehoshua gave life to Rachav, the prostitute. And Yirmiyahu is a descendent of hers and spoke words that were thorns in their eyes (*Yalkut Shimoni* II:15).

The "punishment" shows how slight the charge was. For the reprimanding words of Yirmiyahu had their source in the kindness of Hashem. Hashem wished to bring Israel back to the proper path and avoid the Destruction. If these are the "thorns," the taint which caused them must have been mild indeed. And yet there was a taint and they were punished. Rachav's own lofty nature and gratitude — all these were not sufficient to wipe out a mild taint that persisted and had to be paid for generations later.

(Or HaTzafun I, Omek Chiuvei HaTorah)

⊷§ You Ask for a Ladder?

R' BEN ZION BRUK

Rachav put her life in jeopardy to save the two men whom Yehoshua had sent to spy on the city of Jericho. Even though she belonged to the seven nations of whom the Torah writes, *You shall not allow any soul to live* (*Devarim* 20:16), because she brought herself close to Him, Hashem brought her close. She converted, married Yehoshua, and eight prophets of priestly stock were among her descendants; Yirmiyahu was one of them (see *Megillah* 14b).

Rachav prayed to Hashem: Master of the World, I have sinned in three matters, forgive me these three sins — with the rope, the window, and the wall, as it says, *And she lowered them by rope through the window...* (*Yehoshua* 2:15; *Yalkut Shimoni* II:9).

In her haste to save the spies, after the king of Jericho had sent men out to look for them, there was no better solution than to lower them by rope from the window.

More than eight hundred years later, Rachav's descendant, Yirmiyahu, was imprisoned and placed in a pit filled with clay; he was in danger of dying from starvation. King Tzidkiyahu sent Baruch ben Neriah to lift him out of the pit and save his life. Baruch entered the palace and took tattered clothes. He then went to the edge of the pit and said to Yirmiyahu, *Put the tattered clothes at your armpits under the ropes* (*Yirmiyahu* 38:6-12).

"Would that I had a ladder," said Yirmiyahu.

"You ask for a ladder?" said the Holy One. "Just as your ancestress let them down by the window, you will be treated in the same way" (*Yalkut Shimoni* II:326). Rachav should have set a ladder in place and did not, and you too will have to make do with only a rope.

Rachav saved their lives. By letting them down by way of the window she gained a great reward. But there was a single fault in her good deed: she should have found a more comfortable means of escape. She should have set a ladder in place for the spies and not lowered them by rope.

The Holy One overlooks nothing. That small detail had repercussions eight hundred years later and her descendant Yirmiyahu was treated in like measure when he was raised from the pit.

> Man is measured by the very same yardstick which he uses. [The *sotah*] adorned herself for sin; Hashem makes her look ugly. She showed herself for sin; Hashem reveals... her [hair]. She stood at the door of her house to be seen by him; therefore, the *kohen* places her at the Nikanor gate and shows her shame to all. She put a lovely shawl on her head; therefore, the *kohen* takes off her

shawl and puts it beneath her feet... She made up her eyes; therefore, her eyes bulge... She did her deed in secret; Hashem reveals her in public (*Sotah* 8b-9a).

What we look at as a single act is divided into detail upon detail in Heaven. Each move, each step is considered on its own, and punished accordingly.

(*Hegionei HaMussar, Vayigash*)

⊰ She Who Has Many Children Has Become Unfortunate

R' YECHEZKEL SARNA

The incident of Peninah and Channah teaches us about the depths of Heavenly justice.

Chazal say that Peninah taunted Channah for the sake of Heaven (*Bava Basra* 16a). Because Peninah loved Channah and was concerned lest she remain childless, she taunted her in order to arouse Channah to prayer. She played to the hilt the role of a rival wife.

Peninah was successful. Her taunting caused Channah to pray at length and give birth to a son, the prophet Shmuel. And not just a prophet! Shmuel caused a bursting forth of prophecy where there had been none: *For the word of Hashem was dear in those days; vision was not prevalent* (*Shmuel* I 3:1).

Naturally, Channah was grateful to Peninah. But Peninah had to pay for her act; *she who has many children has become wretched* (*Shmuel* I 2:5). *Chazal* say that when Channah gave birth to one child, Peninah buried two. Peninah had ten children, as it says, *Am I [Elkanah] not better for you than the ten children [of Peninah]?* (*Shmuel* I 1:8). When Channah gave birth to four children, Peninah buried eight. And when Channah became pregnant a fifth time and gave birth, Peninah lay prostrate at Channah's feet and begged Channah to have mercy and forgive her, and the children were considered hers (*Rashi* on *Shmuel* I 2:5).

The punishment was so harsh that Channah's prayer and forgiveness did not help, until only two children remained. The Holy One who examines man's inner workings looked deep into Peninah's heart, did not find a sufficient measure of purity and meted out such a harsh punishment. This shows the measure of Heavenly justice.

(D'lios Yechezkiel II:300)

◄§ You Shall Not Kill

R' AVRAHAM GRODZINSKI

You shall not kill (*Shemos* 20:13). This command seems so obvious that we find it difficult to know why the Torah finds it necessary to write it at all. But upon closer examination we find that the Torah has defined the spilling of blood in a unique fashion.

A man is likened to a killer, if he embarrasses another in public. *Rabbeinu Yonah* classifies public embarrassment as a sub-category of murder (*Shaarei Teshuvah* 3:139). The *Baalei Tosafos* view the act as one of murder itself (*Arachin* 16a). You should throw yourself into a furnace rather than embarrass another. The argument that applies to physical murder applies here as well: Who says your blood is redder than his (*Sanhedrin* 74a)?

As far as actual murder is concerned, the *Ibn Ezra* has written: "You shall not kill" — with your hands or your tongue by giving false witness ... or by giving advice knowing that it will lead to someone's being killed, or by failing to pass on secret information to someone ... which might save him from death... (*Ibn Ezra* on *Shemos* 20:13).

The courts in this world recognize a distinction between direct murder, where a man commits the act himself, and a case in which he is the indirect cause of another's death (*Makkos* 8a). But in the eyes of Heaven, one is guilty for both (*Rashi* on *Sanhedrin* 77a).

How far does this conception of murder reach? *Chazal* say: The Holy One said to David, "How long will this sin be hidden in your hand? Nov, the city of priests, was slaughtered, because of you; Doeg, the Edomite, was banished from both worlds, because of you; Shaul and his three sons were slain because of you" (*Sanhedrin* 95a).

David was not the one who killed them; he cannot be said to have been a direct actor. But he is charged as if he murdered them. For the *Gemara* concludes: The Holy One said to him: "You can have your choice. Either your posterity shall be wiped out or you can have yourself handed over to your enemy" (ibid.).

The very eternity of the Torah demands that every commandment and ordinance be boundless!

(*Toras Avraham, Azharos Sheb'Torah*)

∞ The Trampled Sin

R' CHAIM ARYEH BERNSTEIN

David's behavior towards Shaul was exemplary. Twice he restrained himself and kept his followers from taking vengeance against Shaul, though Shaul was pursuing him. He did not demean Shaul. To the contrary, he recognized him as master and gave homage to him. He spoke with extreme deference to Shaul and honored him as king and father. His attitude of respect serves as a basis for the formulation of the *halachah* that one is required to give his father-in-law the same honor due to his father. When David addressed Shaul as, "My father," this was not an empty phrase; it characterized an attitude of great respect.

But *Chazal* have found fault with even this aspect of David's greatness. R' Yosi the son of R' Chanina said: "Whoever shames clothes, will not derive benefit from them, as it says, *And David arose and cut off the corner of the cloak* (*Shmuel* I 24:5). As a result, *They covered him [David] with [bed] clothes but he was not warmed*" (*Melachim* I 1:1; see *Berachos* 62b).

Besides the charge of demeaning Shaul's garment, we find a further complaint on the part of *Chazal*. Yaakov is described as being angry at Lavan and assailing him. But in fact his words were words of conciliation: *What is my sin and transgression that you have hotly pursued me?* (*Bereishis* 31:36). Yaakov tried to soothe his father-in-law. But David, even as he turned away and refrained from slaying Shaul (*Shmuel* I 26:7-9), nevertheless said: *...But Hashem will strike him, or his day will come and he will die, or he will go down to do battle and perish* (*Shmuel* I 26:10). Men of high stature and nobility sift their speech even at moments of anger. Of them it is said, *He who guards his mouth and tongue guards his soul from sufferings* (*Mishlei* 21:23).

David was punished for his turn of phrase. R' Yehudah said in the name of R' Levi: David let dire predictions about Shaul escape from his lips — *Hashem will strike him, or his day will come and he will die, or he will go down to do battle and perish* — and David was punished for each of these (*Yalkut Shimoni* II:138). His lofty stature required that he prevent himself from speaking the way he did.

Chazal say, "Seven things lie hidden from man and one of them is the depths of judgment" (*Pesachim* 54b). What is hidden includes not only the type of punishment and its magnitude, but also what constitutes a sin and how far a man is responsible for his actions. All this lies hidden. Slight sins and faults which we fail to take note of, or even consider to be *mitzvos*, are included in the indictment above.

> David said, "You have given us 613 *mitzvos* — both great and small. I have no fear on account of the major *mitzvos*. But the minor ones to which men pay scant attention and squash with their heel, those do I fear, for You have said to be as careful of a minor *mitzvah* as a major one." That is why David said (*Tehillim* 49:6), *What do I fear in my days of evil? That the sin of my heels will surround me* (*Yalkut Shimoni* II:758).

It is precisely those sins trodden upon by "the heels" which surround and harm a man.

The pious man who is careful in speech and deed should pray: *You have placed our sins before You, the sins of our youth before the light of Your countenance* (*Tehillim* 90:8). When our sins stand in their nakedness before Hashem and our deeds, which were hidden and covered by the cloak of righteousness and piety, face the light of His countenance, then the truth will out, and we become terrified: *by rage we are terrified* (*Tehillim* 90:7). *Who knows the strength of Your fury?* (*Tehillim* 90:11).

Who can perceive the depth of judgment? It is one of the seven unknowns, hidden from man. Our minds are too weak, too limited, both to grasp the essential loftiness of man as man, and to realize the demands and judgment of Heaven. Heaven judges a man by his greatness!

David, in a moment of great tension, controlled himself and his men from taking vengeance on Shaul. They did not harm him, even though he was pursuing them. Nevertheless, David was charged with committing a great sin by speaking of the spilling of blood. Even though he stood in great danger and his heart burned, this was no excuse. He is reproved because, unlike the forefathers, unlike Yaakov, he did not rise and keep a pure tongue and a nobility of language. He is charged with spilling blood!

This aspiration — to rise to the level of the forefathers — is demanded of each of us. Every man must say (*Tanna D'vei Eliyahu* ch. 25), "When will my deeds reach the deeds of Avraham, Yitzchak, and Yaakov?"

(*Halichos Chaim*).

⪧ To You Alone Have I Sinned

R' MOSHE AKIVA TICUZINSKY

The *Mesilas Yesharim* categorizes David's sin with Bathsheva as a lapse of purity and not as a lapse of care. Care demands that we consider and weigh each facet of an *action*. Purity obligates a man to weigh his every *thought* and calculation to ensure that they are free of any taint of self-interest.

The *Mesilas Yesharim* had a good basis for placing David's sin under the heading of purity. For "whoever says that David sinned is mistaken" (*Shabbos* 56a). Everyone in David's army who went out to war wrote a bill of divorce for his wife. *Rabbeinu Tam* writes that it was not a conditional divorce — i.e. if I should die let this be your divorce — but an absolute divorce which took effect from the moment it was given (see *Bava Metzia* 59a and *Tosafos* ad loc.).

David stood accused only of a sin between man and his fellow man. The entire parable in *Shmuel* of the "lamb of the poor man" (*Shmuel II*,12) is an example of man wronging man. And here, too, David weighed the factors in terms of the honor of Heaven:

> Rava interpreted: What is meant by the verse, *To You alone have I sinned... that You will be right in what You said (Tehillim 51:6)?* David said before the Holy One, "It is known and clear to You that had I wished to suppress my desire, I could have done so, but I did not wish them to say that the servant overcame the master (*Sanhedrin 107a*). [David was faced with a trial and he reasoned that were he to overcome his desire, he would be seen as having triumphed over Hashem.]

But, when all is said and done, David's calculations were incorrect and he is charged with having sinned. Yet, he remained confident that he had acted solely for the sake of Heaven, as the *Mesilas Yesharim* says:

> David took care and cleansed himself completely from anything that diminished purity and therefore went to war with complete confidence... This is what he says in his own writings: *Let Hashem repay me in accordance with my righteousness; let Him give me return in accordance with the cleanliness of my hands (Shmuel II 22:21) (Mesilas Yesharim 11).*

Nevertheless, there remained a taint of impurity and David was charged with committing a sin against another because he wished to sin for the positive sake of the sin.

And the punishment? He sentenced himself: *That man must die and he must return the lamb fourfold (Shmuel II 12:5-6).* Though David was condemned to die, his repentance helped: *Hashem, too, has pardoned your sin; you shall not die (ibid. 12:13).* He did not die; he became a leper instead (*Sanhedrin 107a*), for a leper is considered like a dead man (*Nedarim 64b*). The Divine Presence left him and the Sanhedrin withdrew from him. This too, was tantamount to death; to the wise, a life without Torah is like death (*Rambam, Hilchos Rotzeach 7:1*). He was shamed for his sins until he cried out, "Had they torn my flesh, my blood would not have flowed," for shame is more bitter than death (see *Sanhedrin* 107a). All this was to reduce the sentence of death he had pronounced upon himself.

He must return the lamb fourfold. He was punished through four of his children — the children born to Bathsheva, Amnon, Tamar and Avshalom (see *Rashi* on *Shmuel II* 12:6). If you harm a man by taking and slaughtering his lamb, four lambs must be given up; when it is the man himself who is harmed, one pays with four men. When one robs a poor man, it is as if you have taken his life (see *Bava Kamma* 119a). The parable was about a lamb and he paid with human beings.

But David's punishment was not merely a consequence of the sentence he pronounced on himself. It was a perfectly calibrated punishment. David himself said: *Remove my shame, which I fear, for Your judgments are good* (*Tehillim* 119:39). To which *Rashi* comments: "Forgive me that sin so that my enemies will not be able to shame me. For your judgments are good and I have already taken it upon myself to repay the lamb fourfold."

In addition to this fourfold punishment, David was told: *And now the sword will not leave your home forever. . . I will raise up an evil from your household and take your women before your eyes* (*Shmuel* II 12:10-11).

A sliver of a sin and such terrible punishments, despite the fact that David was constantly remorseful and penitent: *And my pain is constantly before me* (*Tehillim* 38:18); *And my sin is constantly before me* (*Tehillim* 51:5).

David said (*Mishlei* 6:27): "Master of the World, forgive me completely for that sin." And Hashem replied, "Your son Shlomo, in his wisdom, will say, *Can a man fill [the fold of] his bosom with fire and not have his clothes burn?*"

(*Knesses Yisrael* 5749)

✑ It Is Not You
Who Shall Build the House

R' BEN ZION BRUK

David was exceptionally modest. He said, *I am a worm and not a man* (*Tehillim* 22:7; see *Chullin* 89a). "Am I not pious?" said David. "All the kings of the east and west sit in honor surrounded by their courts while my hands are dirtied by blood, by the fetal sac, by the placenta, [so that I can] rule whether or not a wife is in a state of purity for her husband. Not only that, but in whatever I do, I consult Miphiboshes (מְפִיבֹשֶׁת), my teacher, and he tells me whether I have ruled properly; whether I have correctly ordered this man to pay or whether I have correctly declared that this one is pure and that one impure."

"And I was not ashamed" (*Berachos* 4a). The words of *halachah* which came from his mouth, *Mipi* (מְפִּי), caused shame (בּוֹשֶׁת) to David, for there were times when he ruled incorrectly and Miphiboshes told him that he had erred. Because David accepted his correction with humility, he was rewarded with the birth of Kilav (*Rashi* on *Berachos* 4a).

When the Ark of Hashem was brought from the house of Edom we are told: *And David danced with all [his] strength before Hashem... And Michal the daughter of Shaul looked out the window and saw the king leaping and twirling in dance and she felt contempt for him in her heart* (*Shmuel* II 6:13-16). In her opinion it was not befitting for David, the king, to act like a commoner, even before the Ark. And she later reproved him for revealing himself *...like one of the good-for-nothings reveals himself* (ibid. 6:20). Her father's family, she said, had been finer than he. In their day, none of them had revealed a bit of hand or foot, or bared a heel, Heaven forbid. They were all more dignified than he (*Yalkut Shimoni* II:143).

Michal's view can be justified. David should not have shamed himself. The dignified conduct of Shaul, "who was like a one-year-old as far as sin," is indeed a model of how royalty should behave. Yet, what is David's response: *And I sported before Hashem and if I had humiliated myself even more than this, would I feel humble in my eyes (Shmuel II 6:21-22)?* The *Radak* notes that the accent of the verbs is on the last syllables; they are in the future tense. The verse, then, is to be interpreted as a statement with reference to his behavior in the days to come: I shall do more than I have done. I shall dance in joy before Him even more strongly and appear lowly and shameful.

The *Midrash* elaborates on David's response: "Your father's house sought their own honor and neglected the honor of Heaven. I do not do so. I push aside my own honor and seek to honor Heaven" (*Yalkut Shimoni* II:143). David's whole approach was to treat his dignity lightly and to be exacting where the honor of Heaven was involved, even where the issue was not clear cut.

David longed to build a House to Hashem: He vowed: *I shall not come under the tent of my house nor sleep on my bed until I find a place for Hashem (Tehillim 132:3-5). And behold in my torment, I prepared one hundred thousand talents of gold... for the House of Hashem (Divrei HaYamim I 22:14). Chazal* say that David would fast and sanctify the monies which would have been spent on his meals to Heaven (*Yerushalmi, Peah* 4:2); unlike other kings he would limit his meals and set aside the funds saved for sacred use.

It is not a matter of little note for a king to act in such a way. It could be argued that a ruler should adopt the norms of royal behavior. By not doing so, David could have adversely affected Israel's influence on the nations and the strength of her bonds with other kings. But David did not do so; he suffered self-torment and was willing to forego his dignity.

If David did not undertake the task of building the *Beis Hamikdash* until that time when he approached the prophet, it was not from lack of desire. Most certainly there had been no possibility before then to consider the task.

But when he did seek to build it, he was told, *You shall not build a House in My Name, because you have spilled much blood on the earth before Me (Divrei HaYamim* I 22:8). When David heard that, he became afraid and said, "I have been disqualified from building the *Beis Hamikdash.*" Thereupon, the Holy One said, "David, fear not, I swear that I see [the blood] like the blood of a slaughtered deer or stag." *Chazal* interpret Hashem's response in another vein: "I swear that I see [the blood] as the blood of sacrifices." For the verse reads, "much blood on the earth *before Me.*" *Before Me* can only refer to a sacrifice (*Yalkut Shimoni* II 145).

If so, why was David forbidden to build the House of Hashem? *Chazal* reply: You put your honor ahead of My Honor. You asked to be allowed to build the *Beis Hamikdash* only after you were living in your house of cedar wood. But Shlomo, your son, will put My honor ahead of his own, as it says, *And in the eleventh year, in the month of Bul. . . the House was completed. . .* (*Melachim* I 6:38). Only then do we find: *And Shlomo built his house. . .* (ibid. 7:1).

How far Heavenly judgment reaches! Who can imagine the demands which are made? David thought nothing of his personal dignity. He humiliated himself for the honor of Heaven and was willing to make great sacrifices in order to build the House of Hashem. So great was his desire to build the *Beis Hamikdash,* that even though it was his son Shlomo who eventually built it, the *Beis Hamikdash* is referred to as "the House of David" (*Tehillim* 30:1, see *Yalkut Shimoni* II 2). Were it not because of David, the fire would not have descended from Heaven (*Yalkut Shimoni* II 144). And yet, he, himself, was not permitted to build the House because he put his honor ahead of Hashem's and did not arouse himself to build it at an earlier date (*Ramban* on *Bamidbar* 16:22).

A man can lose much that is worthwhile, if he is not as quick to act as he should be. He will be sorely criticized if he first takes care to establish himself and provide for his material needs, and only then turns his mind toward matters of the spirit and the service of Hashem.

We find several references in Scriptures to the fact that David was not to build the House "for Hashem":

> 1) Nasan the prophet tells David: *So says Hashem, "Will you build Me a House to live in? . . .And I will establish your seed after you. . ."* (*Shmuel II* 7:5;12).

2) Shlomo sent to Chiram saying, *You know that my father David was not able to build a House for [the name of] Hashem, his G-d... And now I say that I will build a House [for the name of] Hashem, my G-d as Hashem said..., 'he will build the House for Me"* (Melachim I 5:16,17,19).

3) David said to his son Shlomo, *It was in my heart to build a House for Hashem, my G-d. And the word of Hashem came to me saying, "You have spilled much blood and carried on great wars. You shall not build a House for Me... Behold a child is born to you, he will be a man of tranquility... He shall build a House for Me..."* (Divrei HaYamim I 22:7-9).

Could not David, the pious David, the servant of Hashem have had the proper intention to build a House for Hashem? Was only Shlomo fit for the task? The *Malbim*, I believe, gives the answer:

The main part of the *mitzvah* is not the actual construction itself. It is of major importance that they must build it for [the sake of] Hashem only, without any other intention in mind; without any hope of personal honor or gain. And this is emphasized by the writing three times, *for the name of Hashem, his G-d* (Melachim I 5:17); *for the name of Hashem, my G-d* (ibid. 5:19); *for Me* (ibid.). And, as is known, man by nature finds it difficult to accomplish this. If he expects a great gain, he will not be able to remove all self-interest completely and do it for Hashem alone.

David had already been given a promise through the prophet Nasan. The building of the *Beis Hamikdash* would bring Israel peace from their enemies... He who has a fixed place for his prayers will find that his enemies fall beneath him, as it is written, *And I will make a place for My nation, Israel, and I will plant it and it will rest in its place and not be disturbed any more, and the wicked will not continue to torment it as in the beginning* (Shmuel II 7:10; see Berachos 7b). After David built the *Mikdash*, Israel would have peace from its enemies. This fact made it impossible for David to build the *Mikdash* purely for the sake of Hashem, since he also looked forward to the peace from the enemies who surrounded him, which would accompany the building of the *Mikdash*. Only Shlomo — who began his reign in a era of peace, and of whom Nasan prophesied that he would be a man of tranquility — was able to build solely for the sake of Hashem (*Malbim* on *Melachim* I 5:17-19).

These are words to arouse the true seeker and cause him to tremble. Here we have an interpretation of what "for the sake of" means. And yet, if a Jew gives a coin for charity and declares that he does so in order that his child should live, he is a perfect righteous man (*Rosh Hashanah* 4a). What harm, then, could there be, if David thought, while building the *Beis Hamikdash*, that it would be a salvation for all of Israel and that their enemies would fall beneath them? It would not even have been for himself that he would have had such thoughts, but for the nation as a whole.

We see that even this taints the perfect purity of a thought which is required "for the sake of Hashem."

How greatly a man must labor to purify and cleanse his soul, to examine even his good deeds and subtract all personal interests of honor, pride and gain, if he wishes to strive and reach the wished for goal. All that has been formed was created solely for the honor of Hashem.

(*Hegionei Mussar, Vayakhel*)

᷶ You Have Spilled Much Blood

R' YITZCHAK WALDSHEIN

There are many shades of transgression included in the injunction, *You shall not kill*. There is the "You shall not kill" directed towards the armed robber. And in a far-removed sphere there is the "You shall not kill" which was directed towards David. The Holy One forbade David to build the *Beis Hamikdash* because of the blood he had spilled. *Chazal* say that this refers to his failure to adequately feed the members of his royal table. He rationed the food and put aside the monies saved for the building of the *Beis Hamikdash*. David's purpose was noble: he suffered because the Ark of Hashem was still in a tent, and not in a proper building. Nevertheless, because he did not feed his courtiers as he should have, he was charged with having "spilled much blood."

(Toras Yitzchak, Shevuos)

᷶ Because of a Single Sin

R' YECHEZKEL SARNA

And sinning once, he will lose much good (Koheles 9:18). Because of a single sin, he caused himself to lose much good (*Kiddushin* 40b).

It would seem that all the generations which have gone by and the great leaders of the generations were punished greatly because of a single sin — Adam, because he ate from the Tree of Knowledge; Cain, because he slew Hevel; Avraham, because he asked, "How will I know?"; the generation of the Exodus, which at Sinai achieved the status of Adam before the sin, lost that status through a single sin.

David wept all his days and spent the rest of his life in repentance for a "sin" of which *Chazal* say, "If one says that David sinned, he is mistaken." His sin was forgiven only in the days of Shlomo.

> R' Yehudah said in the name of Rav: [*Chazal*] wished to include another one [among those who do not have a share in the World to Come], i.e., Shlomo. His father's image prostrated itself before them, but they paid it no attention. Heavenly fire descended and lapped at their benches, but they paid it no attention. A Heavenly voice was heard to say, "Will the payment come from your people... Will you choose and not I — i.e., is the choice dependent upon you and not I to determine who has a portion [in the World to Come] and who does not? (*Sanhedrin* 104b and *Rashi* ad loc.)

Nothing changed their opinion until they were told that the matter did not fall into the category of a *halachah* which "is not in Heaven," which depends completely on the rulings of man.

Shlomo occupied the throne of Hashem; he was wiser than any other man; he built the *Beis Hamikdash*. Nevertheless, had the human court been allowed to rule, his single "sin" would have wiped out everything — a "sin," so slight, that *Chazal* say of it, "If one says that Shlomo sinned, he is mistaken."

Nor does this apply only to the great. A man — every man — should see himself standing as if evenly balanced — half worthy, half unworthy. If he performs a single *mitzvah* or if he commits a single sin he tips the balance (*Kiddushin* 40b). The weighing down of the pans of the scale applies to everyone — that single *mitzvah*, that single sin. He may be included among the righteous for a single additional *mitzvah* and thereby gain all that is good. Or he may place himself in the category of the wicked through a single sin and thereby lose everything.

And sinning once, he will lose much good (*Koheles* 9:18).

(D'lios Yechezkel III 170)

⋖ The Act Examined

R' YECHEZKEL SARNA

R' Yochanan said: Why was Yeravam found worthy of becoming king? Because he reproved Shlomo. And why was he punished? Because he reproved him in public. He said to him, "Your father David made breaches in the wall so that Israel might go up [to Jerusalem] for the Festivals. You stopped them up to raise taxes for the daughter of Pharaoh" (*Sanhedrin* 101b and *Rashi* ad loc.).

He was crowned king by a prophet because he fulfilled the *mitzvah* of reproof. But, because that good deed bore a fault, he fell to the point where the verse describes his fate, *to ruin and destruction from upon the face of the earth* (*Melachim* I 13:34). *To ruin* — refers to this world, *destruction* — to the next world (*Sanhedrin* 101b).

⋖ They Deserve to Be Consumed

R' MOSHE TCHENOGEL

R' Ila'a the son of R' Yevorachiah would say: If two wise men walk together and do not discuss Torah, they deserve to be consumed. For it is said, *And it was as they walked and talked, and behold there appeared a fiery chariot and fiery horse, and they separated the two of them, and Eliyahu went up to Heaven in a storm* (*Melachim II* 2:11). They had spoken to one another. Had they not, they would have deserved to be consumed (*Sotah* 49a).

Eliyahu, who was about to ascend to Heaven while yet alive, was walking with Elisha, who was about to witness his master's ascent and who was to receive a double portion of prophecy. Nevertheless, had they not been speaking about Torah, they would have deserved to be consumed. There were no extenuating circumstances.

After such a judgment, what is there to say about how carefully we must use our time in studying Torah?

(Mevakshei HaShleimus 243)

◆§ The Almost Accidental Error

R' ELIYAHU ELIEZER DESSLER

Yehu was very righteous, as it says, *Because you have acted well to do the right thing in My eyes; [because] you have done all that was in My heart to the house of Achav, your sons will sit on the throne of Israel to the fourth generation (Melachim* II 10:30). Yehu slew those who worshiped Ba'al and the house of Achav, after being ordered to do so by a prophet. He uprooted all idolatry from Israel. Yet, in the end he was punished for the slaying, as if it were an ordinary murder: *And I will remember and punish the house of Yehu for the blood of Yizrael (Hoshea* 1:4). And the punishment was in equal measure to his act, because Zechariah the son of Yeravam, a descendant of Yehu, was slain by a conspiracy *(Melachim* II 15:10).

Yehu did not remove the calves of idolatry which Yeravam had set up and thus he did not have the right to kill Achav; he himself did not have hands which were clean from that sin *(Semak, Mitzvah* 283).

We are told how Yeravam fooled the righteous and had them put their seals to an agreement to the setting up of the calves. Even Achiyah the Shiloni put his seal to the agreement.

Yehu was, indeed, righteous. And yet, it is written, *And Yehu did not keep watch to walk in the Torah of Hashem. . . He did not turn away from the sins of Yeravam. . . (Melachim* II 10:31). Why? Rava said that he saw the seal of Achiyah the Shiloni and was misled. *(Sanhedrin* 101b-102a). For this error, bordering on pure accident, he was punished as if he had shed innocent blood. For obeying a prophet, and thereby sanctifying Hashem's name, he was punished as a murderer. The explanation: Had he truly removed idolatry from his heart of hearts, he would not ever have fallen into error.

(*Michtav M'Eliyahu* III:139)

ᴥᔰ His Heart Grew Proud Unto Corruption

R' NOSSON TZVI FINKEL (THE ALTER OF SLOBODKA)

It is said of King Uziahu, *And when he became strong, his heart grew proud unto corruption and he betrayed Hashem, his G-d* (*Divrei HaYamim* II 26:16). Yet, of the same Uziahu we are told, *And he did what was upright in the eyes of Hashem* (*Melachim* II 15:3). [Azariah and Uziahu are one and the same.] His son, Yosam, who succeeded him upon the throne, was said to be good like him: *And he did what was right in the eyes of Hashem, exactly like Uziahu his father* (ibid. 15:34). And of Yosam, R' Shimon bar Yochai said, "If I and my son Eliezer and Yosam stood as a threesome, we would have been able to free the world of punishment from Creation until the end of time" (*Succah* 45b). Uziahu, then, was a man of exceptionally high stature.

In his great desire to come closer to Hashem, he wished to offer up incense. He thought the prohibition against those who are not kohanim — *And the stranger who draws near shall die* (*Bamidbar* 18:7) did not apply to a king. He said, "The Holy One is a king and I am a king. It is becoming that a king should serve before a king and offer incense before Him" (*Tanchuma Noach* 13).

But this reasoning is viewed as the height of arrogance: *His heart grew proud unto corruption and he betrayed Hashem, his G-d, and he came to the sanctuary of Hashem to offer up incense on the Altar* punishment worse than that of Korach and his followers who died in an instant (*Yalkut Shimoni* II:404).

(*Or HaTzafir I, Omek Chiuvei HaTorah*)

❧ In the Midst of a Nation of Impure Lips

R' ELIYAHU ELIEZER DESSLER

And I said, "Woe to me that I am silent" (Yeshayahu 6:5). When he saw the angels praising the Holy One and did not join them, [he suspected that he was not completely pure in heart even when experiencing prophecy and hearing the praise of the angels] and began to feel distress and said, Because I am a man of impure lips (ibid.). He felt that if he had joined his praise to theirs he would have lived forever like them. How could he have fallen silent?

While he stood, still wondering [in deep repentance], he added to his words: and I dwell in the midst of a nation of impure lips (ibid.). Whereupon the Holy One said to him, "You were allowed to say that you are a man of impure lips, because you are in control of yourself. Do you imagine that you rule over My children, that you could allow yourself to say, 'And I dwell in the midst of a nation of impure lips?'" He immediately received his recompense, for it is said: And one of the seraphim flew to me and in his hand was a coal (ibid. 6:6). The word used for coal is not גַחֶלֶת but רִצְפָּה, which stands for רְצָץ פֶּה (crush the mouth), because he spoke maliciously about My children (Yalkut Shimoni II:406).

When Yeshayahu said, I am a man of impure lips and I dwell in the midst of a nation of impure lips, the Holy One said to him, "Yeshayahu, you are allowed to say that you are a man of impure lips about yourself, but you have said that you dwell amidst a nation of impure lips, and meant Israel. They promised 'to do' before they even heard [the commandments] and they take note of My Oneness twice daily in reciting the Shema. Do you dare call them a nation of impure lips?' (Tanchumah, Vayishlach 22).

The Holy One criticized Yeshayahu for what seems to be an exceptionally minor sin — allowing himself to voice criticism of Israel. This teaches us that we are only permitted to look at the good points of another — man is dear because he was created in the likeness of Hashem. We are not to see his weaknesses. We are not to deal with unknowns. Only Hashem can judge a man, for only He can examine the innermost workings of heart and mind. The *Midrash* also shows us that the picture is far from our simple conceptions of things:

And one of the *seraphim* flew to me [this was the archangel Michael, who is the spokesman of Israel (see *Yalkut Shimoni* II:407), with a coal in his hand held by [two sets of] tongs. Why tongs in the plural? The angel went to take up the coal and was burnt. Even Michael is as nothing and can be burned by the fire on the altar where the souls of the righteous are offered up as sacrifices — for they are totally for the sake of Heaven. Michael is the *kohen* who offers up the sacrifices, and nevertheless, though he symbolizes the purest act, strictly for the sake of Heaven, he is burned by the enthusiasm of the righteous who sacrifice themselves for His sake. Michael took up one set of tongs and was burned. [He found it impossible to approach, though he was covered and used an instrument.] He retreated and returned with a second pair of tongs. He held one pair of tongs with the other and took up the coal — now two tongs-length away — and placed it on Yeshayahu's mouth, for it is said: *And he touched my mouth and said, "Behold, this has touched your lips and your transgression will depart and your sin be forgiven" (Yeshayahu 6:7)*. He placed a coal, which he could only pick up by extending two tongs, on the mouth of Yeshayahu, and Yeshayahu was not burned (*Tanchuma Vayishlach* 2).

This was not a sin in the usual sense of the word. Human senses could not find the fault in the action. It was only discernible when brought into contact with the Heavenly fire. And even by Heavenly standards it was a slight fault. Only in Heaven was it possible to discern it at all. By its mere elevation, by having it touch that high level force, the fault vanished of its own. From the earthly perspective, all that the prophet said was an expression of repentance. It was, however, when the total perfection of Heaven above was brought into play — a perfection which escapes even the angel appointed to guard the wholeheartedness of an act — that an excess phrase, the uncalled-for criticism of others, could be perceived. And when the fault was elevated to the Heavens, it was erased, as it is written: *Behold, this has touched your lips and your transgression will depart and your sin be forgiven* (ibid. 6:7). And yet, the consequences were overwhelming:

Menashe slew Yeshayahu. Rava said he judged him and executed him. [Menashe] said to [Yeshayahu], "Your master Moshe said, *For man cannot see Me and live (Shemos · 33:20)*. And you have said, 'And I saw Hashem. . .'" Yeshayahu said [to himself], "I know that he won't listen to what I say. And if I attempt to explain myself, I will turn him into an intentional murderer. [*Rashi*: Because he will kill me anyway, but now, at least, he thinks that he is executing me in accordance with the law.] It would be better to flee." [Yeshayahu would not have fled if he had not been concerned about turning Menashe into a willful killer, for there is something of a desecration of Hashem's Name in flight.]

Yeshayahu said a Name of Hashem and was swal-

lowed up in a cedar tree. They brought the tree and
sawed it. He died when the saw reached his mouth,
because he had said (*Yeshayahu* 6:5), *And I dwell in the
midst of a nation of impure lips* (*Yevamos* 49b).

The impression of the sin remained to the end of his life. For that
reason, the Heavenly name did not save him when the saw reached
his mouth.

As we noted, Yeshayahu said *in the midst of a nation of impure
lips* in a state of repentance. What he said was an unnecessary
expression, but he did not commit a sin. When he came into contact,
in a fiery union, with the powers above, the fault vanished even
when measured by the standards of Heaven, and he was forgiven.
What then remained that prevented a miracle?

Furthermore, the use of Hashem's name is not only a matter of
pronunciation. To express it one must conceive of Hashem as
completely filling all the worlds, and this conception must be fully
accepted in one's heart. With that, one goes beyond the physical
limits of this world, to a state above nature and the sensory world. In
this way, righteous men achieve miracles by pronouncing a Holy
Name. When Yeshayahu uttered a name, he reached beyond nature
and the senses, and his body could be absorbed into the cedar. He
was invisible to someone who looked upon him with a natural eye.
But it was not only that he could not be seen; he should not have
been harmed when they sawed the tree. For just as he could not be
seen, he could not be touched; he was outside the realm of the senses.
Why should his mouth have been affected by the sawing so that he
died? It is to this question that the answer is given. Because he said,
and in the midst of a nation of impure lips.

Yeshayahu could not lift his mouth to the same plane as the rest
of his body which had escaped the influence of the material. It was
not a sin which interposed itself, but an excess expression uttered in
a state of repentance. That had an effect even after he had reached
higher than the angels, and attained the highest of unions with the
Heavenly power, through the touch of the supreme flame of the
spirit upon his mouth. It cast a shadow of the body, albeit a slight
shadow, which could not be detected below at all. Yet it could not be
completely eradicated even by the union at the highest possible

level. There was no possibility of *teshuvah* for it in terms of the body, on the lower levels, because it was so slight that it could not be discerned at that level. And because this was so, it was very difficult to correct it.

But even for such a fault he was judged wanting. For the Holy One is exacting with his pious ones even to the measure of a hairsbreadth. For, have it as you will, the damage was not repaired. Though Yeshayahu might receive atonement and absolution above in the Heavenly *Beis Hamikdash*, his repentance in the world below was not complete.

How can we, lowly as we are, imagine that the outermost form of *teshuvah*, a superficial intellectual or emotional arousal, which does not penetrate inwardly and does not burst forth from the body, will help to erase sins, which are exceptionally great and cling to us like a second skin? Now we can understand, somewhat, why proper *teshuvah* requires such great painstaking care and why Rabbeinu Yonah gives twenty awe-inspiring principles in his *Sha'arei Teshuvah*.

(*Michtav M'Eliyahu II* 282)

↠ One Sin Brings on Another

R' YITZCHAK ISAAC SHER

R' Shimon the son of Elazar said: *Because he said, I have done what is good in your eyes* (Melachim II 20:3). [Chizkiyahu was obliged to say,] *What sign?* (ibid. 20:8). Because non-Jews ate at his table, he brought about the exile of his children. This supports the position of Chizkiyahu that whoever invites an idol worshiper to his table and waits upon him, causes his children to go into exile, for it is said, *And they will take the children who will come forth from you, whom you shall father and they will be eunuchs in the palace of the king of Bavel* (ibid. 20:18).

Rashi explains, Because Chizkiyahu praised himself by saying, *I have done what is good in your eyes*, this caused him to say, *What sign. . .that I shall go up. . .to the House of Hashem?* He asked the Holy One to give him a sign that one sin brings on another (*Sanhedrin* 104a).

This shows us the nature of the sins that are found in those who are truly righteous. Only Heaven could declare what was found wanting in their good deeds and might be called "sin."

When King Chizkiyahu was ill, the prophet Yeshayahu came to tell him in the name of Hashem that he would die. The king said to him, "Finish your prophecy and leave. There is a tradition that has come down from my grandfather that even if a sharp sword rests on a man's throat he should not give up praying for compassion." And when he prayed to Hashem he said, *Remember, I beg you, that I have walked before You in truth with a whole heart and that I have done what is good in Your eyes* (Melachim II 20:3). His pure and truthful prayer was immediately accepted and [Hashem] added fifteen years to his life. Yet, this very prayer, in praise of the good which he had done all his days, and which was favorably accepted above, served as the basis for a charge against him.

It was considered so great a sin that it caused another sin just like it, for he said, *"What sign. . .that I shall go up. . .to the House of Hashem?"* Chizkiyahu's request, too, was accepted on high. That request had been made only for the honor of Heaven and had been meant to spread the word of the kindness of Hashem towards those who fear Him. A wondrous sign was given which stirred the entire world. The shadow of the sun retreated ten degrees, which in turn caused the king of Bavel to seek to know what are the great wonders which the G-d of Israel performs for those who obey His will.

Chizkiyahu rejoiced that Heaven's name had been sanctified in the world through him. He was certain that all would convert and accept the yoke of the kingdom of Heaven, just like all those whom he had freed from servitude to Sancheiriv. They had built an altar and offered up a sacrifice to Heaven. Thus he invited them to his table and exposed them to the greatness which Hashem grants those who fear Him. This was reckoned as a great sin which was caused by the former sins. And for this, Chizkiyahu was punished terribly with the exile of his descendants by Nevuchadnetzar king of Bavel.

Let us look at another passage of *Chazal* which shows us how it was that the evil Nevuchadnetzar was granted permission to rule over Israel and bring great destruction upon them. It reveals something of the mysteries of Heaven and shows the worth that Nevuchadnetzar possessed.

M'rodach Baladan, the son of Baladan, king of Bavel perceived the miracle which had been wrought for Chizkiyahu: the shadow of the sun had retreated ten degrees. He, then, wrote to Chizkiyahu to learn of the miracle. And in the opening of the letter he wrote, "Peace to King Chizkiyahu, peace to the city of Yerushalayim, peace to the great G-d." Nevuchadnetzar was the royal scribe. But he was not present at the time the letter was written. When he arrived, he asked them what they had written and said to them, "You call Him the great G-d and put Him down last. This is how you should write it: Peace to the great G-d, peace to the city Yerushalayim, peace to King Chizkiyahu."

"Let he who has dictated the letter be the one to bring it," they said. [Nevuchadnetzar] ran after the letter carrier. When he had run three paces, Gavriel came and stopped him.

"Because you took three paces for My honor," said the Holy One, "I swear that I will raise up three kings from you, who will rule the earth from end to end."

And these are: Nevuchadnetzar, M'rodach, and Belshatzar. (*Sanhedrin* 96a; *Pesikta d'Rav Kahana*).

A gripping picture. The name of Hashem was sanctified throughout the world by Chizkiyahu because he said, "*What sign...*" and Hashem gave him a sign by having the shadow of the sun retreat ten degrees. The king of Bavel was so amazed that he sent messengers recognizing the G-d of Israel. But this was reckoned as a sin for Chizkiyahu and it caused another sin in its wake: he invited a non-Jew to his table. Because the most perfect of perfect men lapsed once in his life with regard to those messengers, he was punished. His children fell by the arm of the wicked Nevuchadnetzar, who had performed a single proper act; running three paces after the messengers for the honor of Heaven.

(*Leket Sichos Mussar* 289-291)

ക§ Flattering the Wicked

R' SIMCHAH ZISSEL (THE ALTER OF KELM)

Whoever flatters the wicked man shall in the end fall by
his hand. If he does not fall by his hand, he shall fall by
the hand of his sons. If he does not fall by the hand of his
sons, he will fall by the hand of his grandson. For it is said,
*And Yirmiyahu said...to Chananyah... Amen! May
Hashem do that; may Hashem bring about your words*
(*Yirmiyahu* 28:5-6). And it is written: *And [Yirmiyahu]
was at the Binyamin gate and there was an appointed
man in charge there and his name was Yiriyah, the son of
Shelemiah, the son of Chananyah, and he seized
Yirmiyahu the prophet saying, "You are going off to the
Kasdim." And Yirmiyahu said, "A lie! I am not going off
to the Kasdim..." And Yiriyah seized Yirmiyahu and
brought him to the officers* (ibid. 37:13-14).

(*Sotah* 41b-42a)

Chananyah, the son of Azur, prophesied falsely that Hashem
would break the yoke of the king of Bavel (*Yirmiyahu* 28:1-2).
Yirmiyahu "flattered" him, as *Rashi* explains (*Sotah* 41b), by
replying in a very mild fashion. Yirmiyahu should have accused him
of uttering a false prophecy, but instead he said that he hoped that
Hashem would fulfill Chananyah's prophecy. Only then, in the
subsequent verses did he declare the prophecy to be false: *When that
which the prophet foretells comes to pass, the prophet whom
Hashem has truly sent will be known* (*Yirmiyahu* 28:9). But because
he did not expressly say, "You are uttering false prophecy," he was
likened to a flatterer and fell into the hands of Yiriyah, the grandson
of Chananyah.

It is known how much Yirmiyahu suffered for Israel. The

priests and false prophets said that he should be sentenced to death (ibid. 26:11) and he answered, *...Hashem sent me to give prophecy...and behold I am in your hands. Do to me as you see fit and proper in your eyes* (ibid. 26:12-14). Only Achikam the son of Shafan *refused to hand him over to the hand of the people to slay him* (ibid. 26:24).

Hashem commanded Yirmiyahu to place a yoke and its guide ropes on his neck to symbolize the future servitude to Bavel — *Put your necks under the yoke of the king of Bavel, serve him and live* (ibid. 27:2,12) — and he wore the yoke constantly. His life was bitter, *Only to me does He return and turn His hand [against me] the entire day* (Eichah 3:3); *Woe to me, my mother, that you gave birth to me* (Yirmiyahu 15:10); *...because the word of Hashem brought me shame and derision the whole day through* (ibid. 20:8). And then a man appeared who professed to prophesy in the name of Hashem, Chananyah the son of Azur. He broke the pole, the yoke pressing on Yirmiyahu's neck and announced that Hashem had said, *I will again bring to this place the vessels of the Beis Hamikdash that Nevuchadnetzar, king of Bavel, took from this place . . . for I shall break the yoke of the king of Bavel* (ibid. 28:3,4).

Shortly before that, Yirmiyahu had nearly been put to death by the *kohanim*, the false prophets, and the people. Small wonder that he spoke mildly: *May Hashem do that...*" (ibid. 28:6). Although he continued to insist on the truth of his own prophecy, nevertheless, *Chazal* determined that he was guilty of flattery — "Whoever flatters the wicked man shall, in the end fall by his hand." *Chazal* make it sound as though Yirmiyahu was steeped in flattery, though he did nothing more than employ a mild expression when he should have used a harsh one. For that he was bitterly punished: *And the officers were wrath with Yirmiyahu and beat him and placed him in prison . . . And Yirmiyahu remained there for many days* (ibid. 37:15-16).

(Chochmah U'Mussar I:106)

If a Priest and Prophet Be Slain in the Mikdash of Hashem

R' ELIYAHU LOPIAN

*I*f a priest and prophet be slain in the mikdash of Hashem (*Eichah* 2:20). This refers to the prophet Zechariah. What terrible sins were committed: They slew one who was a *kohen*, a prophet and a judge. They shed innocent blood and polluted the Temple area. And all on a *Yom Kippur* that fell on *Shabbos* (*Eichah Rabbah*, Introduction 23).

Zechariah's blood bubbled. Nevuzaradan slaughtered the Great and Lesser Sanhedrin to still the blood, together with young men and maidens, and schoolchildren; but the blood did not cease bubbling. He slew eighty thousand young *kohanim*, and still it did not grow still. How fearful the sin! How fearful the vengeance!

But why did Zechariah's prophecy not save him? Why was he slain because of it? Those who are involved in a *mitzvah* do not come to harm. And in this instance Zechariah was harmed, and by his death he brought death to tens of thousands more.

If the spirit of the ruler arises upon you, do not leave your place (*Koheles* 10:4). *Chazal* interpret this to mean that if you rise in station and assume a position of power over others, do not lose your modesty. And this is meant to teach us that whoever forsakes modesty brings death to himself and sin to his generation. The prophet Zechariah is an object lesson, for it is said: *And a spirit of Elokim clothed Zechariah the son of Yehoyada, the priest, and he stood on the people and said to them, "Thus speaks Elokim, 'Why do you transgress the commandments of Hashem, since you shall not succeed?' "* (*Divrei HaYamim* II 24:20). Did he, indeed, stand on people? The verse refers to the fact that he saw himself as superior to all. He was, after all, the king's son-in-law, a priest, a prophet and a judge. And in this light he said to them, *"Why do you transgress the commandments of Hashem, since you shall not succeed?'*

Immediately afterwards, *They conspired against him and stoned him to death* (ibid. 24:21). This feeling of superiority explains Zechariah's failure to be protected by the *mitzvah* (see *Koheles Rabbah* 10:4).

The taint of pride which infected the prophet was faint indeed; we cannot really conceive it. Even as he was described as full of pride, he was, at the same time, uttering his prophecy. And we are told that the gift of prophecy abandons a man when he is arrogant (*Pesachim* 66b). Though the taint of standing above the people was very slight, it was sufficient to cause him to die and bring about such a sin for the generation.

(*Lev Eliyahu* I:22)

❧ The Wicked Are as if Dead

R' NOSSON TZVI FINKEL (THE ALTER OF SLOBODKA)

Tzidkiyahu was the completely righteous man, distinguished in his righteousness and standing out from among all others of his generation (see *Rashi* on *Yirmiyahu* 38:6). The whole world continued to exist on his merit (*Sanhedrin* 103a). He once swore an oath to Nevuchadnetzar not to reveal a secret. The Sanhedrin annulled the oath with difficulty, for they did so without requiring the presence of Nevuchadnetzar (see *Nedarim* 65a and *Ran* ad loc.). Because of this, we find a very sharp criticism of Tzidkiyahu: *You are a corpse, evil man, prince of Israel* (*Yechezkel* 21:30). He is called both wicked and a corpse. This serves as a basis for the conception that the wicked are called dead even while alive (*Berachos* 18b).

What a difference a hairsbreadth can make. On the one hand, the entire world existed in his merit; and on the other, with the presence of a tiny blemish he is called dead.

(*Or HaTzafun III, Chayei Adam*)

❧ They Did Not Keep the Words of the Elder

R' SIMCHAH ZISSEL (THE ALTER OF KELM)

Heavenly justice is exceptionally exact and precise. No matter how great a deed is, if it nevertheless contains a hint of some failing, no leniency is granted in the Heavenly court of the King of the Universe.

To save a life, the strictures of the Torah are pushed aside. Nevertheless, when the issue involves sanctifying Hashem's name, even human life takes second place. One must suffer martyrdom rather than violate the holiness of His Name (*Sanhedrin* 74a).

The Chashmonaim sanctified Hashem's name for all future generations and established the *mitzvah* of Chanukah so that all might know the great miracle which they had experienced. Yet, they disappeared from the world and whoever says he is descended from the Chashmonaim is a slave (*Bava Basra* 3b). Such was their fate for claiming the monarchy which was destined for Yehudah, as it says, *The scepter shall not depart from Yehudah* (*Bereishis* 49:10).

That the monarchy should remain with Yehudah was not even written in the Torah as a *mitzvah*; we know it only through Yaakov's blessing (see *Ramban* on *Bereishis* 49:10). And even that blessing may only apply when Israel crowns a king and not to kings who assume authority to lead their people in war. Be that as it may, even causing Hashem's name to be known throughout the world did not save the Chashmonaim. The entire family vanished from history "because they did not keep the words of the elder."

What, then, are we to say of one who does not keep the words of the Holy One and whose ancestors are not entitled to great reward for sanctifying Hashem's Name for all future generations!

(*Chochmah U'Mussar* I:126)

⋖ He Shed Innocent Blood

R' YITZCHAK ISAAC SHER

Once two *kohanim* were running up the ramp [to the Altar] neck-and-neck [the winner of the race would perform the morning's service]. One of them pulled ahead and the other took a knife and plunged it into his chest. R' Tzaddok stood on the steps of the hall and said, "Who is to bring the calf which will have its neck broken (עֶגְלָה עֲרוּפָה) — those who live in the city or those in the precincts of the *Mikdash?*" All who heard moaned and wept. The father of the dying youth approached and saw that his son had a breath of life left in him, and said, "He will atone for you; he's still breathing and the knife is not yet impure." [It had not as yet touched a corpse.]

This shows that they were more troubled by the possibility of an animal being rendered impure than they were by the spilling of blood. It was asked, "Had spilling blood become cheap, while the attitude towards the purity of implements had remained unchanged, or had the feeling about the shedding of blood remained as it had been, while they had become stricter with respect to the purity of implements?"

Since they mention the verse, *And Menashe also shed innocent blood (Melachim* II 21:16) [with respect to the incident], we see that it was the spilling of blood which had become cheap while the attitude towards the purity of implements remained unchanged (*Yoma* 23a-b).

T he father, a righteous priest, on the uppermost rung of spiritual perfection, witnesses his son lying before him in the throes of death. Around him, the crowd moans and weeps because of the terrible tragedy which has occurred at the Altar of Hashem. He accepts the judgment of Heaven, like his ancestor Aharon before him, of whom it is said: *And Aharon was silent*. He does not weep or complain. Nor does his attention wander from the service of the *Mikdash*. He is concerned that the *Beis Hamikdash* and its implements retain their purity, that the knife not become impure.

Chazal, however, see him from a Heavenly perspective and find that he holds life cheaply; the spilling of blood is not an overriding consideration for him. This is a frightful flaw in the perfection of his personality. If he had been truly aware, in the full sense, of the horror of [innocent] blood being shed, he would not have noted that the knife had not as yet been polluted. Like everyone else he would have been in shock because of the slaying which had taken place before his eyes.

We are not told that the father did not love his son. No! That was not his fault. We are told that the value put on the need for the purity of implements had remained constant. And that is as it should be. The *kohen* should not feel his paternal love when he stands on duty at his post, as it is says, . . .*and he did not show recognition of his brothers and he did not know his sons* (*Devarim* 33:9). But the feeling of horror at the spilling of innocent blood should have been more intense even than the feeling of love for his son.

A man who had just witnessed such an act should have been so beside himself as to lose all awareness of everything else. He should have forgotten all about fulfilling his obligations in the *Mikdash*, dearer though that is than love for one's children. The strongest and most perfect of souls should have been shaken. He should have become like one who is exempt from fulfilling *mitzvos* because of circumstances beyond his control.

That he retained a grip on himself shows that there was a flaw in his character. Blood was of little consequence to him; he had fallen under the influence of the sin of Menashe, the king of Yehudah, who filled Jerusalem with innocent blood.

(*Leket Sichos Mussar* 291-292)

✍ The Force of Shame

R' YEHUDAH LEIB CHASMAN

Because of Kamtza and bar Kamtza, Jerusalem was destroyed... R' Elazar said: "Come! See how potent shame is. The Holy One gave aid to bar Kamtza, and destroyed His Dwelling Place and buried His Palace" (Gittin 57a)

And yet, who was bar Kamtza? The lowest of the low, an oppressor, an informer. He had no limits to his hatred. His final acts show us what he was like. When he was filled with wrath, he decided to take his vengeance on all of Israel — to kill, destroy, annihilate. Nor was this a decision that was implemented in the heat of the moment. No! There was something of a drawn-out series of actions: he traveled to the emperor; he brought back the sacrifice; he blemished it with his own hands. Can we find a murderer crueler than he?

Chazal tell us that he fell into the category of the pursuer who is chasing another with intention to kill. Such a man may be slain, if there is no other way to save his intended victim. It was certainly, then, permissible to hate such a person. And Kamtza was quite right to eject such an improper guest. But despite all this, because he was shamed, that shame was the cause of a boundless indictment and caused the Destruction of the *Beis Hamikdash*, raging famine and death to tens of thousands of Israel, and the terrible Exile.

Every thinking person will ponder, tremble, and stand in awe.

(*Or Yahel III*)

✥ Acknowledgment of Divine Justice

R' NOSSON TZVI FINKEL (THE ALTER OF SLOBODKA)

When R' Shimon ben Gamliel and R' Yishmael were led out to be executed. R' Shimon cried because they were being executed like murderers. Whereupon R' Yishmael said to him, "Perhaps you were once sitting at a meal when a woman came to ask a question about menstrual purity and the servant said, 'He's napping.' And the Torah says, If you torment [the widow or orphan]. . ., I will slay you by the sword (Shemos 22:22-23)."

R' Shimon remembered that a woman had indeed once come and he had asked that she wait until he tied his shoe. With that he acknowledged the justice of the Divine judgment.   *(Semachos ch. 8)*

R' Shimon ben Gamliel was the *Nasi*, the head of the Jewish community in *Eretz Yisrael*. The woman was a simple soul for whom it was a pleasure and an honor to talk to the *Nasi*. She was certainly not offended by being asked to wait until he tied his shoe. Moreover, such an incident occurred only once in all his years in office.

Still, R' Shimon was judged like one who causes suffering to a widow and, as a consequence, he was executed by the sword like a common murderer. For causing pain to another is a subcategory of murder.

R' Shimon acknowledged the justice of the decree. He knew what punishment would await him in the World-to-Come if he failed to do so.

(*Or HaTzafdin II Musagei HaTorah*).

❧ Woe, If You Would Not Have Seen Me Thus

R' ELIYAHU LOPIAN

R' Nachum Gamzu was blind in both eyes, both his hands and feet had been amputated, and his body was covered with boils. He lived in a dilapidated shack and the feet of his bed rested in basins of water to prevent ants from climbing up onto him.

Once, his disciples wished to take the bed out and then, remove whatever else was in the house. But he told them, "My children, take out the other things first and then my bed, because I am certain that as long as I am in the house, it will not collapse." His disciples said to him, "Rebbe, since you are wholly righteous, why do you suffer such a fate?"

"I brought it on myself," he said. "I was once traveling with a string of three donkeys. One carried food, another drink, and the third various fruits. A poor man crossed my path and came up to me asking for sustenance. I replied, 'Wait until I unload the donkey.' Before I had managed to do so, he died. I went and fell upon him and said, 'Let my eyes, which did not have pity on your eyes, be blind. Let my hands, which did not have pity on your hands, be severed. Let my feet, which did not have pity on your, feet be amputated.' And I was not satisfied until I said that my body should be covered with boils."

"Woe to us," they said, "that we see you thus."

"Woe to me," he replied, "if you would not have seen me thus." *(Taanis 21a)*

He was unloading the donkey. How can he be held blameworthy, if the poor man died before he could give him food? What could he have done?

The Alter of Kelm said that he blamed himself because he should have thought of the possibility that a poor man might happen upon him when the packs were closed. He should have kept food at hand to give to a poor man, until he could unload the donkey. Because he had not thought of such a far-fetched possibility, he called down upon himself a life worse than death — to be blind, to have his limbs amputated, to be covered with boils.

Nor did he consider this a manifestation of going beyond the letter of the law, of piety. He was of the opinion that if he had not sustained such a living death for the rest of his days, he would have suffered far more after death — "Woe to me, if you would have not seen me thus." What can we say? Woe to us, on our day of judgment.

(Lev Eliyahu I 42)

⋖§ His Teeth Were Black from Fasting

R' SIMCHAH ZISSEL (THE ALTER OF KELM)

> *R' Shimon said: "As long as he was alive, R' Akiva felt that [a quarter of a lug of blood made up from the blood of two men] caused impurity. If he changed his opinion after he died, I don't know." We learn that [R' Shimon's] teeth became black from his fasts.*
> *Tosafos: Because it was not seemly to speak of his teacher in this way, he sat and fasted many days. (Nazir 52b)*

He plagued himself so greatly, because he knew that if he did not bring suffering upon himself in this world, his punishment would remain for the next world and the *Ramban* has written that the lightest punishment in the World-to-Come is worse than all the sufferings of Iyov for an entire lifetime in this world.

Make the calculation. If he had punished himself any less, he would have suffered as much as all the pains of a lifetime of Iyov. What punishment would have awaited him compared to the suffering of the fast days which it took to blacken his teeth? And all that for a single disrespectful remark in the course of an entire lifetime. What of the man who speaks improperly in a far harsher manner, not once, but many times each day, and not only speaks, but does forbidden things? Will his fasts and self-torments be enough to extinguish the great fire of the future?

(*Chochmah U'Mussar* I:255).

R' Elazar ben Azariah permits three things and the Sages forbid them: His cow would go out in a public domain [on Shabbos] with the strap between its horns... (*Eiduyos* 3:12).

It was not his cow, but that of his neighbor. Because he did not protest [against its going out into a public domain], it is referred to as his (*Shabbos* 54b).

The *Talmud Yerushalmi* (*Shabbos* 5:4) tells us that R' Elazar's teeth became black from the fasts he kept because of this sin.

This is astonishing. R' Elazar ruled that the act in question was permitted, and he was certainly entitled to hold to his opinion. He should, then, not have been required to protest when others followed it. Nevertheless, his teeth grew black from fasting because he did not inform his neighbor that his fellow Sages felt his action was forbidden. Such a slight sin must be potentially very dangerous if R' Elazar decided to suffer so greatly to cleanse himself from it.

(*Chochmah U'Mussar* II 283)

Blessed is Heaven that It Shamed Abdan

R' CHAIM SHMUELEVITZ

Yom Kippur cannot atone for a sin that a man commits toward another until he appeases the injured party (*Yoma* 85b), and the punishment is terrifying. Abdan, a disciple of Rebbe, affronted R' Yishmael the son of Yose. He became a leper, his two sons drowned, and his two daughters-in-law rejected their husbands. And yet, although this was a frightful punishment, R' Nachman said, "Blessed is Heaven that it shamed Abdan in this world" (*Yevamos* 105b). Compared to punishment in the next world, these dreadful sufferings are like a mere dressing-down.

Not only is the punishment awful, but one cannot argue that his actions towards another had pure motives, that they were for the sake of Heaven. Punishment is a direct result of an act; it cannot be avoided. It is like putting a hand into fire; the hand will surely be burned. Peninah used to torment Channah for the sake of Heaven; she wanted Channah to call out to Hashem in a state of suffering and torment, for children (*Bava Basra* 16a). Yet she was punished with the death of all her children (*Rashi* on *Shmuel I* 2:5).

Rav Ruchami would return home, once a year, the day before Yom Kippur. Once, he became caught up in his studies. As his wife anxiously awaited him, a tear slid down her cheek. At that moment, the floor of the attic where Rav Ruchami was sitting buckled, and he was killed (*Kesubos* 62b). He did not intend to cause his wife grief. And who was it that bore the brunt of his death? His wife who had awaited him. How many tears did she pour out at his death? Nevertheless, there are no excuses when a sin is committed against one's fellow man; the resulting punishment is inevitable.

Binyamin caused his brothers to tear their clothes when the goblet was found in his sack. And many centuries later, his descendant had to make recompense for the suffering caused: *And Mordechai [who was of the tribe of Binyamin] tore his clothes* (*Esther* 4:1; see *Yalkut Shimoni* I:143). Though Binyamin was not to blame that the goblet was in his sack, the punishment could not be avoided. It is built into the nature of things.

The phrase "it was good" does not appear in the account of the second day of creation, when the upper and lower waters were divided from one another. Why? Because Moshe was to be punished on the second day of the week for striking at the rock at the Waters of Strife (*Yalkut Shimoni* I:6). Why were the waters to blame because Moshe was punished because of them? Here again, we see that the punishment for harm caused to another is built into the reality of things; it exists, even if there is no blame.

Anyone who causes another to be punished is not brought close to the Holy One. The *Gemara* contemplates the possibility that the spirit of Navos was driven away from the presence of the Holy One, because Achav was punished through it. Yet Achav was justly punished and the Holy One had sent the spirit to punish Achav. How careful we must be in our behavior towards our fellow men.

(Sichos Mussar 5731:24; 5732:2)

◆§ Those Who Were at the Top Are on the Bottom

R' SIMCHAH ZISSEL (THE ALTER OF KELM)

R' Yehudah was sitting before Shmuel. A woman came in and cried out before [Shmuel]. He paid her no attention. R' Yehudah said to him, "Don't you think, sir, that: He who stops his ear to the cry of the poor man, he, too will cry out, and no one will answer?" (Mishlei 21:13).

"Clever one," said Shmuel, "your head is in cold water [i.e. I who am your head, your teacher, will not suffer for not involving myself in the woman's affairs], but the head

of your head lies in hot water [i.e. Mar Ukva, who is the master of both of us, and the head of the court, will suffer because of the woman's affairs]." (*Shabbos* 55a).

There was nothing that Shmuel could do. Had there been such a possibility R' Yehudah would have told Shmuel to inform Mar Ukva or speak to the woman and explain that he could not help her. But even though Shmuel could not have been of any aid to her, we find that he was punished:

> R' Yosef the son of R' Yehoshua fell ill. He regained his health. "What did you see [when you were lying desperately ill]?" asked his father.
>
> "I saw a world turned upside down," he replied. "Those who are in high position here, were at the bottom, and those who are inferior here, were at the top."
>
> "You saw clearly," said his father. (*Bava Basra* 10b)

Tosafos refers to an oral tradition handed down from generation to generation in the name of the *Geonim* that R' Yosef saw Shmuel sitting before R' Yehudah as a disciple before his master. Why? Because R' Yehudah protested to Shmuel about the latter's behavior toward the woman.

What was Shmuel's sin? R' Yehudah, during his lifetime, performed all the tasks for Shmuel which a servant normally performs for a master. Yet, after death, it was Shmuel who sat before him like a servant before his master.

And this great transformation was a consequence of a one-time sin on Shmuel's part, a sin which we cannot even identify since he could not have done anything to help the woman.

What, then, is the punishment for the obvious sins repeated frequently? Who can picture the depths of Heavenly justice which are hidden from the living?

(*Chochmah U'Mussar* I:160)

⋅৪ Loss of the Kingdom

R' SIMCHAH ZISSEL (THE ALTER OF KELM)

*S*haul was one year old when he became king (Shmuel I 13:1) and Chazal explain, "like a one-year-old who has not tasted the taste of sin" (Yoma 22b).

The Philistines gathered for battle with Israel with *thirty thousand chariots and six thousand cavalry and a nation like the sand on the lip of the sea in great number* (Shmuel I 13:5). Israel fled and hid in the caves and Shaul was left with six hundred men; *and a sword or spear was not found in the hand of the whole nation. . . [except] for Shaul and his son Yonasan* (ibid. 13:22).

Shaul awaited Shmuel who had told him that he would come in seven days' time." But Shmuel did not come to Gilgal and the people dispersed from about Shaul. *And Shaul said, Bring [the animal for] a wholly-burnt sacrifice and the sacrifices to me, and he offered up the wholly-burnt sacrifice* (ibid. 13:9) — in order to pray for victory before Hashem. *And behold Shmuel came.*

Shaul explained to Shmuel, *I saw that the people had scattered from about me and you had not come on the appointed day and that the Philistines would descend upon me at Gilgal. And I had not yet prayed before Hashem and I strengthened myself* (וָאֶתְאַפַּק) *and offered up the wholly-burnt offering* (Shmuel I 13:8-12) Rashi explains אֶתְאַפַּק — "I got the better of my will. For my heart told me to wait for you. But I stopped the [will] of my heart and offered up the wholly-burnt sacrifice."

Shaul stood at the head of six hundred weaponless men. He himself was unlearned in the arts of war — he had been shy and retiring. The rest of Israel was hiding in the caves. Arrayed against him was a huge army, numerous as the sand on the shore, with thirty thousand chariots and six thousand cavalry. Shmuel had not come, though he had said he would. Nor had he informed them that they should wait for him. Shaul's few remaining troops had begun to scatter. At any moment the Philistine attack might come. The only hope lay with Hashem and Shaul therefore wished to offer up a sacrifice. His heart told him to wait, but his sense of responsibility towards his people and his duty as king won out — and he offered up the sacrifice.

And Shmuel said to Shaul, "You have been foolish. You have not kept the commandments of Hashem, Your G-d, . . .and now your rule shall not stand. Hashem has sought a man after His own heart and has commanded him [to be] a leader over His nation, because you have not kept that which Hashem commanded you" (Shmuel I 13:13-14).

Shmuel came and Shaul saw that he had overcome his natural desire in vain, by not waiting. He should have realized, then and there, his error and understood that what Shmuel said, as a true prophet of Hashem, was not subject to change. When Shaul sinned in his campaign against Amalek, if he had immediately said, "I have sinned," perhaps he would not have lost his kingdom. But Shaul felt so bad about the unintentional sin he had committed, that he sought to justify himself and to alleviate his sense of guilt. That is what Shmuel meant when he said, *For rebellion is like the sin of employing magic, and added talk is like error and idol worship* (Shmuel I 15:23) — added words are superfluous; truth can't be changed by words. When he heard that, Shaul understood his mistake and said, *I have sinned* (ibid. 15:24), but it was too late.

That is what is meant by the verse, *And he who admits and leaves off will be pitied* (Mishlei 28:13) — immediate admission and confession of sin help avert the punishment! Yehudah showed that quality. He immediately said, *She is more just than I* (Bereishis 38:26). Shaul lost his kingdom because he tried to justify himself. Yehudah, by contrast, immediately acknowledged the sin and thereby gained eternal rule: *the scepter shall not pass away from Yehudah* (Bereishis 49:10). Such is the difference between immediate and delayed acknowledgement.

How awe inspiring is the exactness of the law, it measures by the hairsbreadth!

(*Chochmah U'Mussar* I:139).

৺ The Unintended
Which Is an Intentional Sin

R' ELIYAHU LOPIAN

R' Yehudah said in Rav's name, "If Yehonasan had given David two loaves of bread, Nov — the city of priests — would not have been slaughtered, Doeg, the Edomite would not have been driven away, and Shaul and his three sons would not have been slain. David would not have found it necessary to ask for bread from the priests of Nov; Doeg would not have told Shaul about it and Shaul would not have died as punishment for slaying the priests of Nov (Sanhedrin 102b-103a and Rashi ad loc.).

Yehonasan is described as *love[ing David] with the love of his soul* (*Shmuel* I 20:17). Their love is the paradigm of love without any mixture of selfishness (*Avos* 5:16); the *Ramban* portrays it as the most shining fulfillment of *love your neighbor as yourself* (*Vayikra* 19:18) because Yehonasan removed all envy of David from his heart and said, *And you shall rule over Israel* (*Shmuel* I 23:17; see *Ramban* on *Vayikra* 19:17).

If Yehonasan was willing to give David the kingdom, can we imagine that he would have denied him two loaves of bread? Yehonasan had saved David from the hand of Shaul. When he saw that his father had decided to put David to death, he sent David away (*Shmuel* I 20:33-42). He did not realize that David had been fasting four days: the day before *Rosh Chodesh* when he had fled from Nayos to Yehonasan, the two days of *Rosh Chodesh*, and the day after when Yehonasan and David met (*Yalkut Shimoni* II:13). Had it entered his mind, he would have furnished him with food. How could he have imagined that his friend had not eaten for three days?

And yet this unintentional lapse is viewed as if it were a wanton sin. In retribution, eighty-five *kohanim* lost their lives; the entire town of Nov was slaughtered — not a child or infant was spared; Doeg the Edomite, the head of the Sanhedrin, lost both his worlds; Shaul and his three sons — Yehonasan among them — were slain in battle.

This would have been a harsh payment for a willful sin, how much more so for one that was unintended!

(*Lev Eliyahu* II:6).